Poeming Pigeons

Poeming Pigeons

Poems about Birds

A Publication of The Poetry Box®

©2015 The Poetry Box®
All rights reserved.
Each poem copyright reserved by individual authors.
Original Cover Illustration & Photographs by Robert R. Sanders.
Editing & Book Design by Shawn Aveningo.
Cover Design by Robert R. Sanders.
Printed in the United States of America.

No part of this book may be reproduced
in any matter whatsoever without written
permission from the author, except in the case
of brief quotations embodied in critical essays,
reviews and articles.

Library of Congress Control Number: 2015933687

ISBN-13: 978-098-6330421
ISBN-10: 098633042-6

Published by The Poetry Box®, 2015
Beaverton, Oregon
www.ThePoetryBox.com
530.409.0721

*To Popo
and bird lovers everywhere*

Contents

Introduction 11
The Invention of Joy ~*Christopher Leibow* 15
Following Leonard Cohen's Lead ~*Karla Linn Merrifield* 16
BirdBath ~*Elizabeth Reninger* 17
Stairs ~*M.F. McAuliffe* 18
Eight Haiku ~*Ram Krishna Singh* 19
Decoding Sparrows ~*Mariano Zaro* 21
Reverse Migration ~*Mary Kay Rummel* 22
Finding Compass ~*Carolyn Martin* 24
The Hajj of Canada Geese ~*Parker Bauman* 26
Hope Between Chaos ~*Stephen Linsteadt* 28
Dawn Over the Bypass ~*Katy Brown* 29
Ornithology ~*Connie Post* 30
Twelve Swans ~*Ariana Kramer* 31
Estuary ~*David Butler* 33
Black Poppies ~*Bobbi Sinha Morey* 34
Secret Poets ~*Darren Donohue* 35
The Language of Birds ~*Linda Strever* 36
Flying: A Poem for Kaeli ~*Christa Kaainoa* 38
A Letter to Thirty Goldfinches ~*Jennifer Kemnitz* 41
First Day of Spring ~*Rachael Ikins* 42
The Robins Have Come ~*Allegra Silberstein* 43
Red Shoes ~*Tricia Knoll* 44
Pileated Woodpecker ~*Sharon Lask Munson* 45
Chorus Lines ~*Vivien Jones* 46
On the Extravagance of a Red-Winged Blackbird ~*Sharon Alexander* 47
Golden Eye ~*Lynn Knapp* 48
If a Homing Pigeon Were My Lover ~*Georgette Howington* 50
Manna ~*Beth MacFarlane* 51
Well Hidden ~*M.J. Iuppa* 52
Owls ~*Davnet Heery* 53
The Wisdom of Birds ~*Jane Yolen* 54
The Crow and I Wait for AAA ~*Lori Loranger* 55
Corvustan ~*Tim Kahl* 56
Bird Bones ~*Marybeth Rua-Larsen* 58
The Unkindness of Ravens ~*Brigit Truex* 60
What the Crows Have Taught Me ~*Donna McLaughlin Schwender* 61
Crows & Keys ~*Eileen McGurn* 63
Scarecrow ~*Pete Mullineaux* 64

The Crows' Field ~*Michael Shay*	65
The Swallow's Tale ~*John Saunders*	67
What They See ~*Shawn Aveningo*	68
Birdlife ~*Susan G. Duncan*	69
Birds ~*Catherine Ayres*	71
Birds as Omens for a Change ~*M*	72
Consequences ~*Gary Beck*	74
Kenspeckle ~*Claire T. Feild*	75
Bird Watching ~*G. Murray Thomas*	76
Breaking News ~*Lylanne Musselman*	77
I Went to a Small Island ~*Gerald Yelle*	78
Blessed Be the Snowbirds ~*Fred Zirm*	79
Bipolar ~*Steve Williams*	80
The Cardinal's Mirror ~*Joan Leotta*	82
Little Bombardiers ~*Marie Lecrivain*	83
Cautionary Grocery Shopping ~*Laurie Kolp*	84
Free Range Chickens ~*Lois P. Jones*	85
Bird Man Does Not Work for Free ~*Alisa Golden*	87
La Semía Paloma's Gift ~*Karen S. Córdova*	89
if i were a pigeon ~*Linda M. Crate*	90
The Small Press Email Bird ~*Doug Draime*	91
Earthbound Wings ~*Melinda Palacio*	92
Birds Over Mainframes ~*Arturo Desimone*	93
Pigeons ~*Cynthia Gallaher*	95
Last of the Passenger Pigeons ~*Mary Jo Balistreri*	98
The Tobermory Dodo ~*Stuart A. Paterson*	99
A Good Day to Become a Vulture ~*Kimberly White*	100
Birds ~*Lytton Bell*	102
Photograph of a Hummingbird ~*Joan Colby*	104
Hummingbird's Mimosa ~*Martie Odell-Ingebretsen*	105
Hummingbird in the Book Store ~*Elizabeth Schultz*	106
Hummingbird ~*Chris Jarmick*	107
Hummingbirds in C Sharp ~*Genea Brice*	108
Counterpoint ~*James B. Nicola*	109
Dal Segno ~*David M. Harris*	110
A New Tune ~*Matt Amott*	111
Coasting ~*Sylvia Ashby*	112
Bird Got My Dreams ~*Madeline Levy*	113
I Kissed You with Sparrows ~*Serkan Engin*	114
Homing Pigeons ~*Todd Cirillo*	115
Homing ~*Deborah Meltvedt*	116
Crusty ~*Judy Darley*	117

Feeding the Birds in a Blizzard ~*Larry Schug* 118
The Safety of Birds ~*Annie Lighthart* 119
Safe ~*Mary Slocum* 120
White Feathers ~*Maria Elena B. Mahler* 121
Wooden Eagles ~*Douglas Spangle* 123
Death by Cassowary ~*Jack Little* 124
China Is Not a Good Place to Be a Bird ~*Lucy Chau Lai-Tuen* 126
Duckling ~*Fern G.Z. Carr* 127
Grieving Mallards ~*Pattie Palmer-Baker* 129
An Alignment in the Yard ~*Sharon Chmielarz* 131
Rock Dove ~*Alexa Mergen* 132
The Business of Caring ~*John Grey* 134
Brown Duck ~*Richard King Perkins II* 135
Bird I Never Saw in Daylight ~*Taylor Graham* 136
Elegy ~*Brenda Taulbee* 137
Matilda Died Today ~*Mercedes Webb-Pullman* 138
The Birds She Never Asked For ~*Maureen O'Brien* 141
Empty Nester ~*Irene Bloom* 142
The Coffin Maker ~*Christopher Leibow* 143
Hot Twelve O'clock ~*Lillo Way* 145
The Sorrowing of Birds ~*Jane Yolen* 146
Impossible Ledges ~*Dianne Avey* 147
His World ~*Moya Roddy* 148
Phoenix ~*Marcas Mac an Tuairneir* 149
Behind the Mountains ~*Hannah Kate Elliott Heltsley* 151
Arrangements ~*Kate Wells* 152
Acknowledgments 155
Contributors 159
Birds of a Feather 179
Bird Index 181
About the Poetry Box / Flight Plans 185
Order Form 187

Introduction

Homing pigeons have been prized for their navigational abilities for hundreds of years. They've served as messengers during war and as a means of long-distance communication. And then along came computers and cell phones. What's a poor pigeon to do? We couldn't help but notice the long line of red feet and beaks-nosing-forward for a better pecking order in the unemployment line. The time has come to help our feathered friends in finding new purpose, fulfillment and job satisfaction. It's time for *Poeming Pigeons*!

Ideally, we'd have a farm of free-range, happy pigeons awaiting their next assignment to deliver love poems to the forlorn, but alas, that wasn't quite in the budget. So instead, we are paying tribute to the homing pigeons of yore with poetry.

For this anthology project, we called on poets across the globe to send in their best poems about birds. And WOW! We were astonished at the plethora of plumed poetry sent to us over the wire. During our submission period, we received over 680 submissions of poetry from six continents. (I'm assuming the ink kept freezing in Antarctica, so it's only natural we didn't receive any poems representing the seventh.) We read each and every poem sent to us and selected just over a hundred poems, paying homage to over eighty variety of bird-species.

As we poured over the poems, we noticed certain recurring themes. The bird metaphors (or 'birdaphors' as Robert cleverly dubbed them) brought to life stories of discovery, innocence, sadness, envy, romance, frustration and loss. It's become quite clear that humans, especially those of the poetic nature, have a deep connection to the world of birds, as illustrated in John Grey's poem, "The Business of Caring" ...

> *... On a regular basis, I attempt to ingratiate*
> *myself into the lives of birds. I keep the outdoor*
> *feeders as well stocked as a bar.*

Now, I have a little confession to make. I've spent almost five decades on this blue ball absolutely terrified of birds … actually anything that flies. About five years ago I began facing my fear head-on and finally reached the point where I could sit calmly among fluttering butterflies and buzzing bees. But when a blue jay came to nibble on my brunch at a lovely sidewalk café in Santa Cruz, I panicked. And forget about walking along the beach with all those seagulls. I was a complete wreck.

And then I moved to Oregon, a haven for nature-lovers and bird-enthusiasts. Magically, it seemed, my ornithophobia began to dissipate. Early that spring, a robin built a nest in our cherry tree and laid four pretty pastel-blue eggs. We named the mama-bird Picasso (because of her unique markings) and watched her rotate and perch upon her eggs. One day, an aggressive blue jay swooped down and attacked, scaring Picasso into fleeing. I ran outside like a mad-woman to chase the jay and save the eggs, but found one gone, one dropped and the last two abandoned. We were heart-broken as we listened to an aria of despair from the birds in the surrounding trees. It seemed the entire aviary community felt this loss.

Weeks later, little black-eyed juncos began to frequent our newly-filled birdfeeder and built a ground nest in the weeds under a pink rhododendron. Every time I walked by, I could hear a panicked clicking noise as the other juncos tried to distract me from the hidden nest. My neighbors probably thought I was nuts as I found myself talking to the trees, assuring the birds I meant them no harm. Soon we had a nest full of baby birds with their mouths wide open, or as Beth MacFarlane describes in her poem, "Manna" …

> *… and beaks spread wide.*
> *Blood red tunnels framed in yellow*
> *open to the heavens,*
> *waiting for their wafer, holy water, manna.*

These moments in my backyard and working on this collection of bird poems has awakened a new passion. I absolutely adore birds! I understand now why my grandfather "Popo" loved to get up early and listen to the birds sing while he drank his coffee. I only wish I could have shared this aviary adoration with him while he was alive. I guess that's why poems like "The Sorrowing of Birds" by Jane Yolen have such a visceral tug on my heart …

> … when the birds are my memory,
> when every morning they sing
> an oratorio to their old friend.

From the bottom of my heart, I want to thank all of the poets who shared their poems, their stories, their heartbreak and their passion for these magical creatures that grace our world and ignite our imagination.

And to all of our readers, I hope you too experience something new through these stories about birds, and like our poet Donna McLaughlin Schwender shares in her poem, "What the Crows Have Taught Me" …

> … above all else,
> always carry your wishbone close to your heart.

~ Shawn Aveningo
April, 2015

 Christopher Leibow

The Invention of Joy

What day was it
that God created
bird song?
And on that day did
the throats of the first
birds who sang, bleed
just a little bit?
Was it on that same day
that joy was invented?
Or that flight became
the home of all those who sing?
Or did the first birds tremble
anxious because of what came
out from their small bodies
did they fear stopping
as if the world would
cease turning?
Or did they fly
higher and higher
singing louder and louder
till they fell back to earth
exhausted?
And was it on that day
that the first falling stars
came tumbling out
of the first evening sky
for all of us
to make
wishes upon?

Karla Linn Merrifield

Following Leonard Cohen's Lead

for Roger M. Weir
with a line from "Come Healing" (2012)

Hallelujah owl — the great horned who-bird
of Everglades pines, magisterial, mythical
by Equinox Eve half-moon, come
to gather up our brokenness on silent wings.

Hallelujah black-necked stilt
skating spring Equinox shallows,
score of more on skinny legs come
to gather up our brokenness, banish the hunger.

Hallelujah storks, hallelujah spoonbills —
woodies and pinkos of Parotis Pond's
rookeries, dozens abuzz as if come
to gather up our brokenness with procreation.

Hallelujah, birds — we fly, we feed, we breed
the wild, our imagination made entire.

BirdBath

only this
matters: this ecstatic
baptism

this standing on stick-
thin legs where the singing
creek pools at the lip
of the waterfall

only this
ruby-feathered
chest diving to meet
its reflection

this beak piercing
again and again that quivering
surface, these wings half-
unfolding, a ruffle

of joy guiding rivers
of light a tumble
of droplets dressed
in rainbows along your hidden
spine

shattering all
decorum beneath
blue branches in quiet

assent ...

Stairs

stairs
of the world:
ant, bush, branch, sun
leaves & cliffs of wind:

beside the stairs
down, around, among
berries —
(continents, car-parks, airports, windowsills)

eyes-wings-cries
mocking boundaries:

& hearing them,
somewhere under my skin my soul
tears.

Eight Haiku

I

between bare branches
two pigeons share silence:
all hallows' day

II

mynahs mate
on the lightning-struck tree:
quiet backyard

III

a bulbul
watching from the snapped twig –
empty street

IV

sparrows couple
on a withered creeper –
peep of day

V

vultures waiting
for the leftovers
of the sacrifice

VI

a cloud-eagle
curves to the haze
in the west

VII

pausing between bites
on the guava tree
the parrots

VIII

a lone sparrow
atop the naked branch
viewing sunset

Mariano Zaro

Decoding Sparrows

My father and I on the balcony
watch dozens of sparrows walking
on the roofs across from us.
A sparrow doesn't really know how to make a nest, he says.
They are messy. Now, a stork, that's different.
A stork makes a perfect nest.

My father looks at the clouds.
Can you tell a male from a female sparrow? He asks.

No, I can't. I say.

Look, male sparrows have a dark stain on the chest,
like a bib or an apron. Females don't.

And I look,
and there they are:
chests with aprons, chests without aprons.
Everything in order.
Clean or dirty,
black or white,
male or female.

I cross my arms against my chest.
My father does not look at me.
And then he says,
But we are not sparrows, you know.

Reverse Migration

It is November in Minnesota
The descent has deepened
from dark to dark beneath
trees that tell us nothing until April.
Work the only way out.

I stay inside as much as possible.
I write. Weavings I brought from
Guatemala help another season
migrate to my house.

Today I pull from the pocket of my journal
a receipt from El Colibri, the hummingbird
shop of women weavers
with pulse quick fingers,
with patience to take two months
to weave a table runner.
Where the Violet Saber Wing
of the Mayan past mates
with the Purple Throated
jewel colors of hummingbirds
of the rainforest.

It is November in Minnesota.
The descent has deepened
from dark to dark beneath
trees that tell us nothing until April,
color being the only way out.
Humming colors,
sun struck fuchsia and orange
trumpet vine shrimp flowers,
hibiscus, papaya, lavender jade,
Green Crowned Brilliant.

Some say hummingbirds
are the moon in disguise
trying to seduce the sun.

Some say the Spanish imposed these designs
to separate the Mayan people into villages.
Women resisted, created new colors that made
the design their own.

Some say hummingbirds
travel all over the world
on the backs of geese.

Steel wings carried weavings to Minnesota
where in November the descent has deepened
from dark to dark beneath
trees that tell us nothing.
The only way out is patience,
the women's pulse quick fingers
the colors that can bring hummingbirds
North in November.

Carolyn Martin

Finding Compass

They look confused —
four flocks of geese
back-tracking routes they flew
southeast last night.
At least, I'd like to think
they are the same —
these squads of Vs,
disheveled and disorderly,
as if a pre-school child
is scribbling lines across
the jagged sky.

Whoever led last night
got something wrong:
mis-read the compass set
for feeding grounds,
mis-scratched the itch to find
a winter home.
The calendar was right,
but something else went wrong.
What is that common saw
about flock leadership?
Weariness requires falling back.
The leader must have missed the sign
or snubbed the call to acquiesce.

Before I wrap my mind
around the science of it all,
one lone goose breaks through
the clouds, driving south-southeast.
A day behind, she missed
their lift-off yesterday,
tonight's impatient flying back.

Against the grain,
a different drum,
and all such idioms
cannot explain
her unrelenting wings.

She's older than the rest,
I fantasize. She's been around
the clouds a thousand times,
knows anomalies of wind,
weather ambiguities,
the myths of leadership.

She doesn't care about uplift
or saving energy to cover ground.
No wingmen or honking cheers.
No urge to lead or tilt
of head as they fly by.

And just as black lines disappear
beyond the Douglas firs,
she strains her neck and lowers
regal eyes — amused, I'd like to think,
by one lone raucous cheer
winging upward toward
the clean-slate sky.

The Hajj of Canada Geese

Just when you think
the world has lost its mind,

you hear them
beyond dusk's cloak

those winged missionaries
evangelizing on silver pulpit.

You can't see them,
oh, but you can hear them;

and you know
that they are scrambling

and flapping
and whisking chaos

into magnificent geometry;
and they call to mind

the ocean's metronomic breaths
and the calibrating celestials.

And in one rapturous heartbeat
they're gone,

those conveyors of certitude,
assailants of amusement

leaving you in bubbling beatitude.
And though

they are the ones
on hajj to a beneficent mecca

you are the one
who experiences salvation.

Hope Between Chaos

A white crane lifts against a grey
sky like hope
between thoughts and borrowed lines
between the crop circles appearing in my unharvested mind.

She calls consciousness and soul into one
where sea and sand disappear
between low hanging clouds.

I look away and fragments of time dip into eternity
between chaos and faith
between rocket launchers and hungry children
between what could have been and what may be.

A white crane lifts against a grey sky.

Dawn Over the Bypass

The wintry sun rises
along a path of shattered topaz

flickering on irregular rice ponds.
A late-rising quarter moon floats

in the violet sky of early morning:
the quietest part of day.

Along the bank of one dark pond
a single egret steps into its reflection

— a lance of ice, watching the water.
From dark salt-grass, a blackbird

tries to call back the season
in the untamed tongue of wild song.

The silent miracle of a dozen cranes,
necks outstretched,

wings beating in unison,
flies in a low, ragged vee

— their red caps brilliant
in defused light.

Some counsel on the wind
over the great sand hills

set these birds in motion
ahead of the wall of winter.

Ornithology

I want to freelance
in the eve of birds

not fly, or soar
or carry the strength of wind

I want to know
how to find the thin power lines
how to balance
when the flock
leaves you behind

how to identify
the noises of departure

I want to know
how to find the distance
from branch to soil
how to atone
for the loss of gravity

I want to learn
to become an unencumbered silence
and extract autumn
from each weary leaf

I want to be statue-like
in the depleted dawn

I want you to understand
why I bathe myself
in the ruined twilight

Ariana Kramer

Twelve Swans

Falling
            slowly

                        down

twelve swans fly to their sister.
She does not speak. Her fingers cold
with worry and the nettles' sting
fly up in recognition, fly up to their
small heads, long necks, plump backs.
Their *honk, honk* subsides to soft clucking.

That night, after they have flown to the wild country
she closes the door to the warm castle, steps barefoot
into the garden, kneels before the artichoke, holds
its bloom close to her cheek. The downy inside
the prickly cover

                familiar

                familiar

                familial

To break the spell that keeps her brothers swans,
she gathers nettles near the graveyard, weaves them
into shirts, stays silent. For seven years she works
embroidering fine stitches with the sting of blood.
A witch, the townsfolk say. *Does not speak.*
Eats her children. They nod. They tie her to a stake.
She does not say a word. When twelve birds alight
she lifts the fabric in her arms. Twelve nettle shirts
finished but for one, fall on the feathers of brothers.
The air rushes with wind, the people look in awe.
The birds turn to human form, only the left wing
of the last brother remains, without a sleeve.

Youngest Brother keeps his wing tucked against his breast.
The smooth, wide feathers lift of their own accord
when the wind is right. At night, he settles against
his magic limb, covering eyes with snowy softness.
He always drifts into sleep cautiously, as if dreaming
is a hidden thing, to be hidden. He always dreams
of nests, the feeling of flight in cold, winter skies.
He never tells her he is sorry she made the shirt.
If he could he would give up his arm to be a swan.

This poem is based on "Six Swans" and "Twelve Brothers," German fairy tales collected by the Brothers Grimm, and on "The Wild Swans" by Hans Christian Andersen.

David Butler

Estuary

Daylight drains into the sea's radiance.
The mackerel sky can no more retain it
than we can hold the moment. Now,
light lies in shards on corrugated mudflats
where all day, a party of oystercatchers
darted like animated sewing-machines
to tack down the tidal filigree.
Now the mudflats are empty.
Dusk has begun to silt up, and you'd think
the place could not be more desolate,
when a curlew's ululation reverberates
beyond a heron's hunched endurance
across the inconsolable sunset.

Black Poppies

Stars are hiding tonight,
the raven dressed in
mourning, singing to me
of a fluttering veil of a
roving widow. He pecks
at the rope above me,
woven by tears and
oblivion, depositing his
secrets in my sordid ears;
his feathery wings like
black poppies I cannot
look at without dying.
In the moonlight, he
watches my last bitterly
joyous exertion, the shape
of fear inside my heart,
which trembles and endures.

Secret Poets

Like a symphony of
Secret poets
They convened
Nesting on a masterpiece of
Spider web branches

Ashen clouds
Bark and feather
Each perfect
Synapse hopping to and fro
Like the birth
Of some beautiful thought

With a climax
Beyond me
They rise
Sending the air spinning
Leaving the tree to mourn
The loss of so much life

The Language of Birds
  ~ *for Lois*

More than once I've asked for a sign.

I've asked mute air and sky how to find
you after you pass from this life.

Today a mourning dove crashes into
the window, sits stunned on the deck —
her soft body, her whispers of color —
and I get it now, watching her recover,
watching her sweet head, her shining eye.

She lifts to the feeder, coos, and another
dove flies in, struts and bobs on orange feet.
They feed together quietly, dip into
the birdbath undisturbed, as if to offer
ease on this day, the last one before

you'll begin your leaving. Tomorrow
you plan to stop exactly what the doves do
now — eating and drinking — so you can slip
the rest of the way out. Yes, you'll come
to me in birds, and I realize I've known it

since last summer, just after you were
diagnosed. Startled by a thud, I went outside
to find the blown-glass garden ball lying
on the deck, whole, an opalescent mirror
for the sun. Two ravens circled low over

my head, and I had to smile at the brightness
they'd tried to steal. Yesterday in the woods

I laid my palm against a cedar tree. Two band-tails burst from its branches, and I glimpsed the white curve of their rising.

Flying: A Poem for Kaeli

Black crow perches on the top branch
of the tallest fir tree,
secure amidst the swaying limbs.
Cocking her head left, then right,
her ebony eyes observe the terrain below
and she calls out,
a long, sharp Ka --- Ka---

Beneath her, on the sidewalk,
I pause to listen to the familiar greeting
of my avian neighbor.
We seem so different,
she – untethered,
and I – so utterly terrestrial,
but we breathe the same air,
and my skin brushes the same wind
through which she flies,
and I live on the same earth as she,
and so do you,
the thought of which, in this moment,
floods me with warm gratitude and joy.

Ka --- she calls again,
"Eli!" I shout into the sky.
Ka --- she calls,
"Eli!" I return.

And for a few frozen moments,
she and I, together,
sing the song of your name.
Sing it like the Hawaiian spirits did
before you were a seed of consciousness,
before your parents lived,

before their parents lived,
when only spirits lived,
and they called you,
Ka-eli.
Called your name into the wind
knowing that it would ride
the tuberose breeze into the future,
an opal incantation,
a promise of breath,
your breath,
your flesh,
your wings,
the spirits called you into being, Ka-eli.

And here,
millenniums later,
this crow and I sing your name, together,
call and response,
Ka-Eli
Ka-Eli.

You are Here!
Part of me,
part crow,
part spirit,
part parents,
part dusk of evening,
muddy blue sky pink smudge,
part crisp autumn air
and rising half moon.

The promise of days
of love,
of life,
a destiny,
unfolding fulfillment.

Crow sings Ka ---
I shout "Eli!"
Crow sings Ka ---
I shout "Eli!"

Never mind this city street,
this broken sidewalk,
this passing neighbor
who can't hear this song.
Even the crow herself wonders
what and why I sing to her,
but I know,
and now you know ...

Time does what time does ...
Crow spreads her wings
and flies from the fir tree toward the moon,
black wings extended,
eyes set ahead on the horizon.

Jennifer Kemnitz

A Letter to Thirty Goldfinches

Dear Garden Foragers from Ten to Noon,

You butter birds spread atop the crisp
Of seed-paper spires, a literal charm,
I am pleased and obscurely proud to host you
At this lunch the earth and I made with light.
Just the old miracle: lustrous sustenance
Partaken by all, whether bone-treed
Like us, carapaced, or spongiform.

Yet, when I see you at my pantry,
That bountiful board of lemon balm fronds,
Onion ball puffs, anise hyssop popsicles,
Favored, plumpest-aphid-haunted sunflowers,
And hear your soft, sweet, feeding "tsee,"
I'm embarrassed to admit a particular fondness,
A warmth I wonder if you could ever fathom
Even if my words could leap into song
And cross the gulf between Mammalia and Aves.

And could I ask, is it okay to enquire —
Might you love me also in your fleet way?
Perhaps some glancing, uninvolved ardor
Like the trees' for the sky, the sky's for the earth,
And the earth's more than

Cordial,

Almost affectionate,

Regard for,

Me

Rachael Ikins

First Day of Spring

Flocks flutter in on ragged edges,
winter's tattering wing. Don't pay
the cold any mind as wind freezes
tears pulled from your eyes.
Close them. Listen to the celebration –

Exhausted voices' jubilant declaration
"We are here. We made it. We are here!"
Redwing blackbird males tricked out,
black satin tuxedos with red/gold trimmed
epaulets. Inky blue speckled starlings

wheeze and rock, toes clamped to
tips, poplar wands making magic
with unseen sun. Buds swell this gray
day. Robin males chortle and plaintive
3-note melodies of grosbeaks,

dark velvet jackets, white waistcoats and
a dash of scarlet at the throat. Cardinals whistle.
Chickadees three note enticements. Threaded
through sparrow arguments and catastrophe.
Wheeling gulls spoked in sky cry. Silhouetted
hungry hawks, tails a rustier red to catch

the eye of a lone female. Takes her time.
Slaloms through snow flakes without
moving her wings at all. Gusts shred,
swirl winter›s feathers.
Spring bustles in.

The Robins Have Come ...

they are everywhere
on the lawn
in the trees
a marvelous multitude.
They feast
on pyracantha berries
and full and fat
defy my cat
intimidated perhaps
by so many red breasts.

Red Shoes

Red shoes are hushed-up woman-secrets —
stilettos, lace-up sandals, ballerina flats,
garden muck-outs, ankle boots, fur-trimmed booties,
toeless pumps, running shoes, sneakers
in closets, scuffed like promises.

Tipping a pair of red shoes, girls dance,
prance, romance. The vain fairy tale
princess craved red shoes. She got them.
They danced at her mother's funeral
and drove her insane.

Laugh at the lowly pigeon hen,
strutting the curb, seeking cooing from her cuddles.
She's a grand wannabe girl on parade,
waddling on tiny red feet.

The little old lady on the bench
tossing dry crusts wears red shoes too.

Pileated Woodpecker

He works with a vengeance —
claiming territory
this crow-sized bandit
tap, tap, tapping
his beak, a chisel and crowbar

hammers away, non-stop
perforating cedar siding
off my clapboard house.

I shout, raise my voice
wave arms, clap hands
consider stapling netting to the eaves.

But when I catch flashes —
black body, red crest,
zebra-stripes down his sides
I am stunned into silence.

My maneuvers, interrupted.
Gazing in admiration
I am trounced.

Chorus Lines
Caerlaverock

>Barnacles in black stockings,
>Bewicks minus mascara,
>Mutes in white feathers,
>dancing in on splayed kite feet,
>Mallards roughing up the girls
>while the wigeons whistle,
>
>Here come the noisy ones,
>In dull dun plumage but,
>Oh boy,
>in pink shoes and lipstick
>*anser brachyrhynchus*
>steal the show

Sharon Alexander

On the Extravagance of a Red-Winged Blackbird

"He does not think himself common."
~ Cornell Lab of Ornithology

As though the male knows
his glossy obsidian feathers
ignite his epaulets into flame.

As if in flight his span
of wings could brighten
the eye of every aviator.

As if in perching on a sign that reads
"Palmdale Fin and Feather Club"
he is playing tricks on us.

As though Van Gogh dipped his brush
in cadmium red and splurged the last
of the tube on those wings.

As if the delicate way in which
he balances on a swaying cattail
is his treatise on ballet.

As if his reedy song could help but call
to mind Coltrane's soprano solo
on "My Favorite Things."

As though he doesn't know how splendid
is his trill — a choir of chimes colliding
on a silver cord.

 Lynn Knapp

Golden Eye

I sprint up the wildwood hill,
snowy path stretching ahead —
tic-tac-toe of animal and human,
cat, dog, Nike tread,
magpie alighting,
running steps of rabbit.
A solitary pheasant, a young male,
clatters out of the brush,
flying alongside me
until his fear is spent.

Perhaps he is lost,
separated from his family
or in search of one.
Ah, now a slim brown hen
scuttles into the undergrowth.
The rooster is not searching for a hen;
he has found her
and shelters her in the thick brush
on a snowy slope
of the freeway.

As I crest the hill,
not one trim brown hen,
but two run at my approach,
and there he is again, that handsome devil,
turning a golden eye toward me,
lifting emerald head and crimson throat,
leading flight to a brown-twigged hill
across the rusty railroad track.
I stop, breathe deep, and hear
the rattle of their wings,
sense the pounding of their hearts

and count,
not two, but three, then four speckled hens
raising wings to follow him.

Georgette Howington

If a Homing Pigeon Were My Lover

Fluffed and preened on the shelf
I could not help but notice
your bobbing head and piercing eyes
twisting and turning to see if I was
looking at you the way you looked at
me in that wanting way as if my
human form was a pigeon too.
How unlike me it would be to take
off into the sky, fly across the expanse
in circles feeling the wind, gliding on
our wings, not arguing about who did
not fold the laundry, or if I am too tired
to have sex tonight or being pressed
to spend time with family I don't like
and living from moment to moment
dining on seed offerings from the keeper
moving aside to let him do all the
cleaning and arranging of our coop
while all you and I do is fly, eat, and
think about making baby pigeons ...

Manna

The shell is tapped from the inside
with the egg tooth,
a raised bit on the beak
used like a tiny hammer.
"Break glass in case of emergency."

The hatchling hears the mother bird,
knows it is time
and begins to tap its way out.
Fissures spread, light slips in.
Some mothers eat the shell fragments
their new chicks step from.

Some eat their babies,
but never for no reason.
It's the siblings one needs to fear.
Crying, pushing, peeping, wriggling.
The runt may get tossed or crushed.

They throw their heads back,
thin nubbled necks stretch taut
and beaks spread wide.
Blood red tunnels framed in yellow
open to the heavens,
waiting for their wafer, holy water, manna.

Well Hidden

    Snooping under ivy, curly
    and thick, we disturb
    a sparrow's nest, no bigger
    than a measuring cup
    full of fidget.

    Tiny gray heads tilt
    upward with eyes shut
    tight — tongues fluttering
    like monks in ecstatic
    prayer, offering their hearts
    to this day that has begun
    with us eavesdropping
    on their cloistered life —
    their sole contemplation.

Owls

There they were,
two of them perched,
a pair of mops on a branch
or a couple of banshees,
their grey tendrils
hung out to dry.

They sat soundless and still,
their black bean eyes
beady in skull-sockets;
their beaks flattened
to heart-shaped faces,
ghostly in the grey light.

They seemed benign,
and they drew me in.
While I held their gaze
not a moment moved,
nor breath exhaled,
no pulse throbbed.

Now, I'm full of owls:
ten at least on my torso,
six or seven down my legs,
and more on each arm —
Commedia dell'Arte masks
cover me all over,

and their characters
are peering through,
but I don't know
who they are,
where they come from,
or why they're here.

Jane Yolen

The Wisdom of Birds

> *"Animals are often smarter than people, so it is they who should object to anthropomorphism."*
> ~ John Hornstein

The wise owl, or so he's been dubbed
by some anthropomorphic admirer,
looks down from his tree
where he's been contemplating
the square root of shrew.
Giving a small cough, he throws up
a bit of wisdom, shaped exactly
like a pellet, stuffed full of bones
and fur.

Not exactly Schopenhauer,
remarks a nearby crow,
though he knows how to satisfy himself.
The mob flies off laughing,
whether at the owl,
now considering his flight feathers
and the phenomenon of mice,
no one can say, wisdom not
being the forte of crows,

though they have snark down pat.

lori loranger

The Crow and I Wait for AAA

Triple A is late
But the crow waits with me.
I didn't notice her at first,
up in the tree that's been shading me —
magnificent trunk
I can't get my two arms around,
deciduous leaves and clusters of seed pods.
She cawed then, just to let me know
I wasn't waiting alone
and tipped her head to one side
as if baffled by why
I would wait for one machine
to haul off another
rather than just taking wing.

Tim Kahl

Corvustan

They came armed with their neophytes and
pamphlets to my door, pressing me about
my readiness for the afterlife. I wasn't ready.
There was still some preening of my résumé to do,
and amends to make for the times
I'd thrown *The Watchtower* straight into
the recycling. All those smiling faces
accepting Armageddon unnerved me.
I was pretty sure I wasn't going to
get in, past the checkpoints where
the purity of soul was measured.
But I read for them out of their texts
every Thursday afternoon. I was a user-friendly
starter kit for the new recruits to practice
their lines. I admit their zeal amused me;
I answered earnestly at first,
but as the cars whizzed past and
the birds began to gather, I succumbed
to the pressure of being rude.
I told them I'd seen God on video at
the downtown library. They could go
there and check it out if they wanted.
They sensed I was being less than honest
and challenged — do you even believe?
You see those four crows sitting on that wire.
I believe . . . they're angels, secret angels
that report everything I say and do
to the old master crow back in Corvustan.

In Corvustan, the old master was the best talker,
every caw and coo practiced as a call to assembly.
They arrived in line for the night roost to gossip
and grab each others' bills, a line of flying birds

seven miles long. They mobbed the owls in the day,
and knocked a squirrel out of a tree with
dive bomb bravura. A random head of wild red hair
was singled out for scolding. Then during downtime
at the roost the old master began the debriefing.
But aren't the best talkers also the best liars?
Hadn't the ancestors spoken the truth about
the best food always coming from following armies?
Certainly this was as true as old Noah's crows feeding
on the floating corpses. Kid Corvid agreed and
retold his riddles of caw and countercaw,
the parable of the ant in the feathers,
the intractable problem of the tug-of-war with
a twig. Au-Pair-of-the-Air put on her clinic of
soaring and tailfanning, her acrobatic dives
and rolls. They all talked at once. They all
took turns talking, but none could explain
why they still met on this paved spot on
the backlot that used to be a dump full
of so many delicacies. Rewind to last Friday when
the sentence came down and the mob growled
its opinions. They considered the spectacle of
death and the purity of the soul, how ready-to-wear
the afterlife is. The condemned one was
marched to the end of the branch, and then lay
crumpled on the ground, neck broken.
While the mob lifted up en masse and silently
flew away, away — a murder of crows.
Ah, sweet Jesus, this harbinger of death —
There's a murder of crows at the end of the world.

Marybeth Rua-Larsen

Bird Bones

You were born with bird bones,
strong, hollow, light enough

to let you fly, like the crows
on our maple who squawk and scatter

with every honked horn
but return in the quiet,

determined to stay. I've read
crows study faces, remember

what we do, hold us accountable,
and I hope your memory

is shorter,
that you've forgiven me

my one long strand of hair
wound around your newborn

finger, turning it blue,
the grief it took us

forty-five minutes to find,
stripping you naked, unraveling

the cause of all
those tears, and I know

what the crows know: that we line
our nests with the bones

of our ancestors and the fallen,
defending our murders,

pulling them deeper
into our folds.

Unkindness of Ravens

It may have come from long ago,
when first Raven stole the sun
and left the world to wither and shrink,
for necessary movement
to slow perceptibly, cease
altogether.

Or so it seemed. Of course, fire
was retrieved, rekindled. Of course
there was a hero
to salvage the world. The thief

bears the evident scorn —
char of feathers, smoke-
rasped voice, the gravel of coughs
and croaks. So where

exactly is the unkindness
placed, on the gathering of
these sooty scoundrels, mocking
in their strut and badger, their
immemorial need for
the ignescent core of creation?

Will they one day burst into
a radiance of color, all that is
compacted within that cinder-
coal body with wings? Will they
scale their way upwards, their songs
rising like smoke?

Donna McLaughlin Schwender

What the Crows Have Taught Me

Don't be in such a hurry
to distance yourself from your family.

Finding a lifelong mate
really is possible.

Be faithful to your own flock,
but never hesitate to help others in need.

Stand up to bullies,
regardless of their size.

Being part of a murder
can be a good thing.

Take turns being the lookout
for those you love.

When communicating, keep it simple
and be loud enough for others to hear you the first time.

Heed the warning calls
of those you trust.

Being called an old crow
is actually a compliment.

Black really is beautiful
in every form.

Life is a balance of being grounded
and knowing when to take flight.

Being big-boned
doesn't impede one's ability to fly.

The width of your wingspan
doesn't determine how far you'll travel in life.

Don't be afraid to change course,
even if it's at the last second.

Fly,
even if you don't excel at soaring.

Don't let anyone tell you otherwise —
hopping is a legitimate mode of transportation.

Sometimes,
strutting is required.

If a tool you need doesn't exist,
be resourceful and create one.

Never underestimate
the intelligence of others.

Accept handouts graciously
and share the bounty.

Stop being wasteful —
eat the damn leftovers!

And above all else,
always carry your wishbone close to your heart.

Eileen McGurn

Crows and Keys

Song in the forgotten style
Call more tradition than stubborn luck
You land out back
Perch on an abandoned piano
Scratching the warped wood
Raven soars on flat wings
You on feathers bent back up
The piano is backless, tuneless
Broken and peeling
Scarred ivory and cracked veneer
The wind thrums a low beating hum
On rusted strings
Some sprung
Like every jail that tried to hold you
Lock picker
Scrambler of secrets and laws
You break out
Like you break codes
With a blink of your black, black eye
Then turn to the uncertainty of flight
Obsidian risk

Pete Mullineaux

Scarecrow

The cheek of those crows! He squints out at dark scavenger birds
invading the surrounding fields following incessant rain. To which
a voice from above replies — *Crows? Who can tell a rook from a raven,
daws from doves at this distance? Get out there man, this instance —*

engage with the enemy, let's know what we're dealing with.
So, rituals completed and venturing out before the flock
hastily gathered in rough assembly, now somewhat depleted,
he takes time to ponder, to note: amidst the uniform, a motley

coat — grey beak here, clean cut nape there, two shady hoodies
in conference by a stone wall; seven magpies, (he counts them all.)
Some plump wood-pigeons coo, a cut above the rest. Then feeling
a chill on his chest and shifting feet to ease the circulation, he

sees them fidgeting too in relief; recognises old mischief in Rook's
ragged trousers, cheeky Daw's two-footed skip; it breaks the ice,
forces a smile to the weathered lip; welcome respite for a wintered
soul, hungry for seasoning, some good old spice. Turning to go

he raises a hand without a second thought to a sudden awkward itch
inside the collar, hears a great 'whoosh' —
        they are airborne!
The very earth churning upwards, a dark storm spiralling above him now:
raucous mass of unintelligible chatter …

And for a moment it doesn't matter, the field is his. He stands alone
staring skywards, wingless and bewildered. Though some are soon
returning in scooping reconnaissance, re-alighting on the old stone walls,
phone wires; all eyes on the next signal: watching, waiting.

Michael Shay

The Crows' Field
~ *for Vasko Popa*

Crows gather in the park
Old men around a bench
Or maybe children
Hopping from swing to slide
Picking at letters
Someone had left behind
For the squirrels

Pecking at the odd vowel
Or gulping the wet morsel of consonants
With an upward slash of their matt beaks
They wait to scatter
Until the last possible moment
Whenever two legs or four
Come too close

They fight off the bigger gulls
Who glide above
From an ocean too far away
Gulls who are never completely comfortable
Forced to the old baseball fields
Between the fiction of infield sand
And the rhythm of grass

Nipping in frustration
At the divots of sharp syllables
The gulls are disappointed by the leftover pieces
A slash or a broken V or at best
An abandoned semi colon

The crows even intimidate
Small syllables of dogs

With their secret knowledge and black longings
On the ground
They do not speak to each other
Unless fighting over a moldy word

But once in the air
They call out
Sharp slogans
Maybe in the joy of flying
Maybe just to clear the way
Into the open sky.

John Saunders

The Swallow's Tale
(After Philip Larkin)

    My kind has a certain reputation,
    messengers of God's displeasure
    who herald misfortune for you.

    We are cited in proverbs and poems,
    share a myth about passing through a room,
    have earned a crow-like mystique.

    It is late summer, time to migrate,
    the whole sweep gets flighty,
    a sort of pre-flight tension.

    I leave my flight to watch you take
    a photo, point at me or stare,
    and wonder what you are thinking,

    how it feels to be grounded,
    you a prisoner of evolution
    like us, winged or unwinged.

    Perhaps we are not so different,
    for I have watched your kind
    dash down lanes and overtake.

    You fly and crash into each other,
    your dead bodies found on the ground.

What They See

When the birds watch
us,
what do they see?
Do they make notes
in their guidebook:
Identifying Humans for Dodos?

> The man with the bulbous red nose,
> they name *Mr. Booby*.
>
> *Look! It's Ms. Peacock*,
> they squawk, pointing to a woman on stage
> as she dances behind her fan of feathers.
>
> They observe the odd behavior
> of the one they call *Penguin*,
> wondering why she strikes a stick
> across the hands of the youngling.
>
> They compare notes, confer
> to determine why a fair-skinned hen
> nags and pecks at her colorful partner
>
> and which one really did
> come first?

One by one,
the segregation continues,
based on mere appearance
they separate us

from our flock,
as we do ourselves,
from human
kindness.

Birdlife

It wasn't enough
    to ply them with

           thistle
           sunflower

at strategically
    placed feeders,

to whisper their
    common names

           and Latin

inside the window —

she perched their
    ceramic cousins

           barn owl
           chickadee

on the mantel.

      But once aligned,
rarely remarked.

          I'd guess a
            nod to
           fairness —

from this

vantage point

                dining room
            breakfast nook —
family feeding,

          bird, watching.

Catherine Ayres

Birds

Sparrows perch on a bare tree
like raisins spiked on a fork.

Rooks use a copse as a trampoline

and a blackbird pulses across the lawn,
full of blind intent.

A seagull makes a white sail in a grey sky
but geese go one better and make a V.

A hen looks up through its monocle,
missing everything

and a pigeon shits on my car.

Plus ça change, sighs the owl.

Birds as Omens for a Change

April 22: we sputter outside a MiniMart
in my sister's planned community near Baltimore.
Inside, you argue with the Pakistani owner
over hot dogs, maps. Maybe you were Hart Crane
in a former life. How you'll decide
to end this one is questionable. The motor

is running; quick escapes are your M.O.
Simon and Garfunkel kick around
the radio; a fabricated pond, too many
trumped up trees stand on my right-hand side.
Hire Rasputin to direct set design
and this is what you get. I am looking

up. Two western grebes soar,
swoop, dive, shampoo, rinse, repeat
around the pond.
They are off-course. Six years

ago precisely, a wasted merlin,
not aquatic, veered, dived;
ill-timed syncopation. A bridge, troubled water
laid him down. I bowed my head
to that alliance, kept it low
through the interment
and years of sidewalks
where the only change I bummed
was made of mercury or wood.

The grebes hesitate, flick wings,
run on water more miraculously
than a god who merely walked,
completely immerse, then lift.

With head bowed, I would have
missed this. You return to our car.
I look you straight in the eye.

Consequences

Only humans use the word
proliferation,
but life forms seek it,
successfully for some,
diminishment for most.
I see this daily on my terrace
where birds gather at the feeders.
The flock of alien sparrows
denying small birds a meal,
intimidating the cardinal
who's just not strong enough
to resist barbarian hordes.
The blue jays and mockingbirds
disperse the little gangsters,
but are chased by the pigeons,
large flying creatures
that live openly in cities
tolerated by people.
The robins are unchallenged,
but always feed cautiously
wary of man the provider.
Many beautiful native birds
are being eliminated
by unregulated immigrants
more adaptable
to changing conditions,
urged along by meddling men
ignorant, or indifferent
to the fate of feathered friends
doomed to extinction
by thoughtless disregard
of their right to life.

 Claire T. Feild

Kenspeckle

He lives within vines watching soreheads make unsettling mistakes. By being alone, he avoids the camaraderie with patience he needs to be happy. But he fears meeting others because he thinks they will organize a sortie as they laugh at his ungainly freckles he carefully carries around as if they are scorpions trying to move. He is afraid of the facile smiles at his kelly green cap speckled with red mudlets and their clownish finger-points at his shoes having holes filled with socks that look like toasted bread. The night the slight winds feel to him like nature's guidance, he leaves his post of contagion, letting his shadows bud on roads he will travel down since he decides to not care what others think about the awkward presentation of his wares. Within his conspicuousness, he is surprised, for others embrace his diversity as if he were nature's new species of hummingbird.

Bird Watching

A flash of feathers in the brush,
too swift to attatch a name to,
but enough glimpse of brilliant plumage
to create the possibility
of a startling new bird.
None of the standard manuals
list this species.

But what is this need to identify?
As if, without a name,
the bird does not exist.

Relax.
Enjoy the glorious,
unfamiliar song.

Lylanne Musselman

Breaking News
(After the painting 'Birds and Pears' by Natalie Strand)

Envision
it: Instead of the latest arson

that killed a mother and child,
or the newest story of corrupt

police officers, pitiful politicians,
or lethal child bullies, the breaking

news interrupts The Biggest Loser:
Rare and beautiful birds

have been discovered in Indianapolis –
they remind birdologists of an American

Robin in size and continuous cheery song,
but what baffles are their intricate markings –

the flamboyant birds are striped like a rainbow.
The birds were found in a crook of a tree

that pairs branches of fragrant pears. Poets and artists
from around the world are flocking to this tree –

armed with edgy words and brazen palette knives.
It appears the blameless have a chance to recoil

from the damage that evil snake caused
when coaxing the innocent Eve to bite

into that seductive skin before anyone else
could.

Gerald Yelle

I Went to a Small Island

    in the Aegean where flightless birds
    navigate rivers and streams
    like penguins but with three times
    the number of nerve endings
    and capillaries in their fins.
    They communicate while swimming:
    a cross between signing and telepathy.
    You never hear them coming.
    They're just there putting
    thoughts in your head. I heard
    they could help break negative habits.
    Help you quit blaming yourself
    for evils you didn't cause.
    I heard people quit smoking
    after swimming with a bird that flapped
    its fins at a rate that mirrored
    the echo of the human heartbeat.
    I spent a month hoping
    they'd fill me with endless cheer.

Fred Zirm

Blessed Be the Snowbirds

No, not the ones that flee to Florida but
the ones that stay and brave winter's last
storm and sing, though the dawn be dull
and flake-filled, they believe in the
calendar and not the cold.

Yes, I know their songs may be more
battle cries than lullabyes, bragging
of what they have and wailing for what
they want, but that makes their singing
no less beautiful, merely more real.

Maybe they are winged Whitmans
singing songs only of themselves, but
they sound more like they're rejoicing at
the dying of the night, and this dark
morning, they have sung me into song.

Bipolar

After a blizzard of rain,
the bicycle storage
is flooded. The fire alarm is shrieking,
and the elevators are closed.

You climb the steel stairs –
the ones that say 'roof access here.'
Find the lever
next to the meter
that turns off the gas –
shut it down.
Light a match in the fog,
go to the edge, measure the stories
in the tunnel between you
and the dumpster
squatting on the asphalt
like a peeing dog.
You talk romance
to the mourning dove
on the balcony across the street –
you're sure she loves you.
Take a fried egg
sandwich out of your pocket,
share it with a crow
before she takes it.
You are 15 minutes from flying.
You've flown here before.

It was 4:00 a.m., all the birds were roosting
except this crow.
And the garbage trucks
were clanging iron
while you lit a match.

All the crow wanted
was the jewel
in the tunnel
of your left eye.
If you had a will
or note, you'd leave it to her.
But then, she's a crow
and can take it
before you blow it out.

S and M at Nye Beach

Between parking lot and tide,
finger-thick cables
stretch through a fence
of concrete pillars.

One is occupied by a watchful gull
as a second floats above her,
starts to land on her head.
The first gull is still,
never looks up,
then wings down a single stroke
and drifts over
to the next open perch.

I say, pecking order or maybe,
like at airports,
the bird in the air
always has the right of way.

She just laughs,
confides that no,
it's love.

Joan Leotta

The Cardinal's Mirror

As I climbed my steps,
I saw a puff of red feathers
on the porch,
surrounded by a swarming of ants
feasting on the once-living cardinal carcass,
once a pretty bird
now reduced to insect food.
I reflected. Probable cause of the bird's demise?
He must have seen himself,
mirrored in our door's storm glass,
seen himself as a sleek, crested rival
flying toward him.
Enraged, he flew against it in attack. He lost.
I sighed. I understood.

When I approach that wicked glass,
an older, heavy woman often
steps out toward me.
She holds my purse and packages
in her arms.
I admit I've considered attacking her.
Now, seeing the bird's result,
my aggression dims. I'll
make peace with the crone.

After all, she has to clean the porch.

Marie Lecrivain

Little Bombardiers

The early risers
who sip coffee,
fold towels,
and hang up
button-down collared shirts
on plastic hangers
don't notice
the row of pigeons
strung on an electrical wire
above the laundromat,
the fully-stocked
soap dispensers
or change machines
ready to accept
their hard-earned cash,
until they arrive home
to find a Kandinsky
or Rorschach masterpiece
on their freshly-laundered clothes.
And so, they make their way
back to the laundromat,
now crowded
with working mothers
and their truckloads of wash,
pause beneath
phone wire
now empty
of little bombardiers
and wonder ...
    and wonder ...

Laurie Kolp

Cautionary Grocery Shopping

There's no easy way to say
I was shit upon today
while walking out of the grocery store
all nonchalant-like, without care, almost bored
minding my own business, strolling along
when I heard a PLOP in my hair so long
and felt a warm goo, like an egg or a splat
looked up like a fool, I was just beyond that
awning where pigeons nest in red letters
the storefront's façade, birds perched
as if waiting … prepared to squirt
their shit on the first housewife they see;
how could this happen to me?
I stopped in the drive, asked a lady to glare,
was there something in my hair up there?
Much to my WOW with her finger she swiped
the splotch on my head, right on the side.
She said it was sticky, revealed brownish crap,
I gave her my cart wipe to use with a snap.
Then she stroked it all over my bird-nest hair
and befuddled, we walked away from there.

 Lois P. Jones

Free Range Chickens

> *"Oh give me a home, where the Cornish hens roam*
> *and the cock is chained to the chicken coop."*
> *~ Anon.*

Last night at the grocery store, just a hair before 9:00 p.m.,
when the security guard stood like a Dade County Sheriff
at the electric doors, I squeeeeeezed in and made a dash
for the dairy. Skated my way like a roller derby queen, dodging
the dilatory cart holders — you know the ones that put their load
dead center in the isle. There's no room to push past
their cart and a staredown to the back of the neck
is as pointless as well, lipstick on a pig. Aggressive manoeuvres
may get you hounded (yes I was once pursed by an angry shopper
somewhere between canned veggies and caramel corn rice cakes).
So I pushed the cart ever so gently out of my way and made
a quick break for the eggs — my last chance for a morning
protein to go with the ever perfect latte, and lo and behold
there were those free-range chickens.

Now you know what I'm going to say. That's right, them hens
had holsters and metal guns and they was a whoopin' and a hollerin'
and riding their little chicken-sized horses in a big circle, firing
their cap guns into the air and the smoke was clouding up
the entire dairy department until the organic cows began to promenade
with their big milk carton placards 'EMANCIPATE THE PRISONERS!!'
up and down the black and white tiles, as they chanted
free Daisy now, free Daisy now and they got louder and louder
until the bacon stood up on its end, real lean and mean like
and shaped itself into a long lasso circling and circling
just above my head. I swear the whole damn store was ready to riot!
I began to run for my life, toilet paper rolls unfurled at my feet,
brooms and mops fell in front of me, sacrificing their lives,
angry bags of popcorn exploded at random! I swore if I made it out

I would let the world know the truth:

Free range chickens (do not) roam the countryside, writing poems and discussing God, glad to lay their happy eggs.

Final line from David Callin's poem "I should pay more attention."

Alisa Golden

Bird Man Does Not Work for Free

Bird Man on the pier: darkly tanned, strong-armed. On his bike
perch five bright birds, all different, all talk. In his hands, the birds
fold up. He tosses them sky high,
like footballs.

The first camera out is the trigger for the show: this woman has
a very big lens. Bird Man takes his cockatoo and leads it
to her shoulder. The bird, white-crested, sits on her
embarrassment. Gives her a kiss. And preens.

Alert, his eye roves, catches the next cameraman,
snaps a colored parrot to
this man's arm.
Bird Man's hatched a statue: face red, feet suddenly stone.

While they simmer, Bird Man stays away from strollers,
hooks a beak on some teeth: green beard hanging.

Say cheese.

Scanning still, he spots a third: a woman aiming right at him.
Unhooking Mr. Parrot he
puts him on the husband's head:
the perfect souvenir shot.

Bird Man zooms in, takes back the cockatoo, accepts a five-dollar bill,
scoops up the parrot, staring, waiting for the frozen man;
the last couple scrounge three bucks between the two of them,
give him back the green bird, the green bills, and two nods.

Credits roll.

Bird Man is attractive. He attracts crowds.

So many tourists in summer, all ages.
Reaching out of strollers, fearful fists of desire open and close.
Wanting, not wanting. Everybody wants.

Fly.

Karen S. Córdova

La *Semía*: Paloma's Gift
Taos, New Mexico

I thought I only stopped
for gasoline at Taos Chevron,
but then I saw a banker's flannel
pigeon pecking, picking at the ground,

head down, hungry like an accountant
searching for a penny —

its beak-tapping rhythm focused on scent
of seeds like an auditor's fingers scratching
for seeds of cents by masterfully,
mindlessly rapping on a 10-key pad.

I saw bird as accountant, quivering
head especially, and elegant
tremolo with purpose. I wanted him
to sprout a black-tie tail,
but he was gray.

Unlikely suitor
glowered at my rude interruption,
protected something like a glowing opal
in his translucent jowl — or, perhaps,
swallowed a purple sunset on a stormy day,
and I caught him in the act.

He left a gift. It was here
in a rental car (a Taurus)
on Paseo del Pueblo Sur
that I began to write.

Linda M. Crate

if i were a pigeon

if i were a pigeon i
cannot help
but wonder what message
would i carry?
one of light and love or one of
disillusionment and distance?
would i be a long
epiphany scribbled out on a piece
of paper almost too long for
me to carry or would
i be a piece of paper with words
left unspoken?
would my message be something
anyone would like to hear
or would they see
me coming and cringe once removing
the paper from my leg —
if i were a pigeon
then i'd like to fly high in the heavens
close to the sun
see if i couldn't burn the wax off
fall into the sea
kiss the ocean for but a moment before
the predators could strike
before flying into
the oblivion of a sunset
returning in the morrow with another message
perhaps this one more sweeter than
the last.

The Small Press Email Bird

The small press email bird
is a very rare and shy bird,
seething with fear and unrequited love.

It lives camouflaged among the
palm trees, sycamores, and
the weeping willows. Fair warning:
they must be approached
with extreme caution and gentleness.

The wrong word in an email, or any honesty
or directness whatsoever, a boo or
a *brusque* movement, and they
will fly, fly away never to be seen
again. Many of them have flown
away from me, I am sorry to admit.

And ole brash me not understanding the
seemingly bottomless depths of their
sensitivity and paranoia, which motivates
their quirky, turtle-shell behavior.

Expressing my dissatisfaction in general
with email communications, and asking
for (maybe) a phone number, or to meet them
personally one on one, for a beer or coffee,
gets not a peep or tweet in response.

I have emailed Capistrano more than once,
hoping to learn of their return fluttering down on
delicate wings, along with the beautiful swallows.
And I am happy to report that the swallows have
returned again, but unfortunately no sign of the
pouting and fragile small press email bird.

Melinda Palacio

Earthbound Wings

We set our sights south, we sisters
who never knew our father's homeland, Panama.
My sister decides she will wear a gold figurine as talisman.
The harpy eagle, national bird of Panama, represents all our ancestors.
The shop keeper decides Emily needs gold feather earrings.
My sister, a golden goddess, released of earthly goods and dollars, can fly.

On the last day of our trip to the land shaped like a curved snake, we see
a harpy eagle, more majestic than expected for a bird of prey almost extinct.
My sister squeezes my hand. Within seconds,
the bird folds her amazon wings to land on concrete.
We think she might speak to us.
Perhaps tell us the meaning of life.

The raptor offers nothing, not even a squawk.
Instead, she swoops onto a discarded Happy Meal.
Collar and crown open, an owl face scrunches in disappointment.
McDonald's fries smell better than a juicy sloth for a second or two.

My sister snaps a photo, posts it on Instagram, Facebook, and Twitter.
Emily turns her earthbound wings on the largest raptor she will ever see.
When words of wisdom fall like rain on a hot day, the harpy eagle is
too far away. We hear only a faint sound from her hooked beak.

See me, see me, see me.

Arturo Desimone

Birds Over Mainframes

If we still knew how
to train birds
to send and bring the letters, warrants,
papyri to fear or anticipate,
declarations and refusals of love,
subpoenas —
then we wouldn't ever need to mainframe
Only to leave little indentures
and stone bowls full of water,
some seeds and Attarsheya flowers
for the birds, like what Arabs leave
for their mother's graves
in cemeteries of dry dirt under sun
And every third window
would be busy
with birds coming and going,

No one would squabble over computers
virtual telegrams
all of us transistor-mechanics on flat bureaus,
reading one another's morse code
faceless blank books

Instead of a send-lever
we would dispatch the message
by kissing the bird on its head,
read throat, thumb on picking beak,
then throw it at sky's cloud-brains
that never fall or cease dreaming
and our message would not
crash or fall to die in the wingspan
of its own dirt-hugged shadow

Effort is necessary to pick
the fastest bird,
the prettiest,
or the most gray, depending on
the nature of the message
and the beauty of the recipient:
orange black Troupial, who sings sweetly,
the Caribbean Chuchubi, gray and hoarse
who announces death by blue-tailed grape lizard
African Swallow: faster than mercury
the merchant
of financial underworlds,
he holds the legal codes of Cupid
speeding through the treetops
where violets grow over the wet cemeteries
and the hammocks of passion's recipients.

Pigeons

> *"Pigeons are the spics of birdland."*
> *~ David Hernandez*

Bright messengers,
who mess our church roofs,
you've been replaced by voice mail,
leaving thousands of you jobless,
loitering in the parks.

It wasn't that way
when they sent one of you
in each of the four directions,
telling the world Ramses II
was the new pharaoh of Egypt.

It wasn't that way
when Nero sent your kind
to his friends
with news of the latest
Olympic sports scores.

It wasn't that way
when Brutus released you
by the cages full
across opposing lines,
with messages to Mark Antony's army.

It wasn't that way
when Rome considered you a delicacy,
fattening you by the thousands
with bread softened
by the chewing of slaves.

It wasn't that way
when Moslems
set up a permanent post
for you in Baghdad,
the world's first airmail service,
or when Christian armies intercepted you,
using only the most merciless weapon,
the peregrine falcon.

It isn't like you're forgotten,
today's science lab whiz kids
discover you grasp
the meaning of "people,"
"trees," "fish," "oak leaf,"
   or "human being"
between your pigeon-toes.

It isn't like you're endangered,
we don't stalk you
for your pomegranate tongues
or warmth-bearing robes,
no landfill has turned mass grave
for your two-pound bodies,
but along city streets you continue to stand,
like the 1500 applicants gathered
for 19 post office jobs.

It isn't like you've completely lost it,
there's one breed among you
who'd fly 100 miles per hour,
600 miles a day if need be.

Perhaps we just don't pay
attention anymore,
and you imitate us
as a last ditch
for our wingless embrace,

multiplying in our urban spaces,
pecking at loose concrete or odd garbage
as we do at keys of our computers.

Perhaps you've grown dependent
on our ancient praise,
on our continued hand feedings,
and on memories of a once great era
that yearned for pigeon-delivered gossip.

Perhaps it all started
when we sent you out from the ark,
   like a sacrifice to an empty sky,
   like a burnt offering,
(if it hadn't been so blasted wet outside)

and you hovered over the earth,
in a sky as blue and blank
as a freshly-scrubbed ceramic bowl,
never knowing if you'd drift back home
to our lonesome ship,
our tiny sliver-like flaw gliding
along a seamless ignorant shadow,
but with olive branch as proof,
you returned a message to our motley payload
of endangered species,
"Land, green and swelling,
with a juicy rumor of tomorrow."

Last of the Passenger Pigeons
~ *for Martha Washington*

The heavens turned pale when dear Martha died,
sang singer John Herald in words that decried
the loss of the wild once sweeping the land
for passenger pigeons the vast sky spanned.
A phalanx, a fleet, now extinct worldwide.

The thrum and thunder, the fast-flapping stride
climbing the clouds, day-darkening the skies —
massive migrations. Imagine how grand!
Once billions, then none when dear Martha died.

They forage cornfields, the trees they shanghai,
their dung falls like snowflakes, men would reply.
Their voices grew strident, rife with command,
It's us or it's tem, thus mass slaughter began.
Too late the codified laws multiply.
The heavens turned pale when dear Martha died.

Stuart A. Paterson

The Tobermory Dodo

Whit's yon ye say?
Ye've ne'er heard
o Tobermory's
wingless burd?

Yin day it grew
gey seek o copin,
up't an skriegh't fareweill
tae Oban,

flew tae Mull
a while tae bide,
loast the baith its wings
an steyed.

Alas, it ate
jist Cullen Skink
an twae year later
went extinct.

Glossary:
Oban – west coast Scottish port lying opposite the Isle of Mull, of which Tobermory is the main port; **burd** – bird; **yon** – that; **yin** – one; **gey seek** – very sick; **skriegh't** – screeched; **bide** – stay; **loast** – lost; **baith** – both; **steyed** – stayed; **Cullen Skink** – famous Scottish smoked haddock & potato broth; **twae** – two

 Kimberly White

A Good Day to Become a Vulture

We have watched each other these last few days, years. Me,
repulsed by the death on their breath, attracted to their eloquence

them,
attracted by instinct

> *Sharp shoulders hunched, droopy necks sway, they are unbothered
> by beating sun. At night, their presence is even stronger than when they
> are in full daylight view*

I hide in the shade.

> *Dawn shows, black to blue then red at the line, massive wings blue-
> black flecked with rusty red stir the currents of morning air*

I have put on a red dress to match their wrinkled skin.
They eye me from all angles, judge my velvet vanity

In dreams, I wonder how it would feel to wear their skin as my
own, see a vulture's face look back from the mirror, see me
wear vulture wings

> *Unafraid of me, they flap their wings, hop and bob their necks, nip
> at each other with clattering beaks*

> *restless after a motionless night*

stretch myself out, stiff and new, feathers crinkled like a newborn,
ungainly in the new day, unstained by the daily mire

heavy wings split the layers of air, slip through stratums of blue violet
white

> *below, Coyote hunches his shoulders and bobs his neck
> tries to look like them*

> *but even Coyote will step back in respect when the flock comes down*

The circle tightens

Small hungry sounds cut the air. Down below, something dies. Air
bleeds with the scent of adrenalin, pumps with the struggle
between worlds

then the odor of death as it succumbs

> *Coyote takes a sniff, then defers to his place in line*

One by one, drop from the sky, take positions, begin the grisly dance.
Ravenous. Long curved beaks snap and salivate

no thoughts no decisions, just Vulture being Vulture. Claws dig for
leverage, beak sinks into flesh, blood still warm covers faces
already red, drips from chest and wing feathers

nothing ever tasted so good

> *Crows coyotes and other scavengers wait their impatient turn*
> *Coyote tries to sneak in, hunches his shoulders and bobs his neck,*
> *puts on his very best Vulture face*
>
> *backs away as soon as Vulture shows him some fangs*

Upon eating our leisurely fill, the remains are left to the others. Rest,
digest, clean leftover bits of flesh from messy feathers

sleep our Vulture sleep while the lesser carnivores devour what is left
behind

In Vulture dreams, layers of blue-violet air ripple red-stained wings,
glide among changeable blues, lazy whirlwinds circle down to the call
as the hand of Death sets the table down below.

Birds

They bug me
While others sigh over them, writing flowery poems
I think of how their white, chunky, gloppy shit
coats everything: newspapers
caked into the bottom of golden cages
my windshield; my long, freshly shampooed hair
that used to smell of strawberries and limes

A little kid once died of West Nile virus
simply from touching one of their molted feathers
he found on a path in the park
Dirty, disgusting, hollow-boned, mean spirited little fuckers!
No wonder they are angry

My daughter, enraptured
on spying a river gull soaring through the air
whispered: "Wouldn't it be amazing to be a bird?"
So I told her about Icarus and his painful fall
Better to be anything, even a lowly plankton
than to spend your days hovering in a blank sky

Why am I not jealous of flight?
Birds are beautiful, right?
They whoosh, zoom, dive, and swoop
They sip sugar from feeders with their pointy beaks
From their perch among the branches, they sing and sing
weaving silvery ribbons into the twigs of their nests
swiping a tender wing over their clutch of bright blue eggs

When they see me coming, they hunch like vultures
blocky in the winter trees; stark reminders
of all the risks I could not or would not take
Their wistful tweets turn into accusing caws

I saw a dead baby bird once when I was eight
limp and rotting just beneath our mulberry tree
It tried to fly too soon, my mother warned

So today I amble along the cliff's edge
my shoulders itching, staring
down the sheer rock face into the sea
The birds are walking now, not flying
But I see their wings
And they see mine

Joan Colby

Photograph of a Hummingbird

It hangs like a furious angel, blood throated,
Stiletto beaked, the astonishing thirst
Of a brutal metabolism
As it prepares to assault the hydrangea.

This is not the way we like to think
Of a hummingbird. Its sovereign ease above
A fount of nectar. Little bird, hovering like the
Possibility of paradise. This photo

Limns a darker intensity: the surge
Of lust when the rapist decides, when the poem
Stabs into the corolla of the mind
And sucks it dry.

 Martie Odell-Ingebretsen

Hummingbird's Mimosa

Above a Mimosa tree
with flowers going to seed,
dripping down pink
to the ground, green;
hark, the stir of wings.

Holding on to air
is the quickening sound;
don't dare interrupt the flow;
make quiet your watch, not caught.

The dignity of a spear
assaults the flowing tresses
bunched and pressed there;
leaning into the drifting breeze,
cuddled in quiet wait to fall from tree.

Lithe with zip-twirl,
the road an airway;
it supped at bird-stop,
filled-up with sweetest fuel,
then stopped before my wonder-face
and dared the air between us,
then was gone.

Above a Mimosa tree,
holding on to air,
the dignity of a spear
lithe with zip-twirl ...
hark, the quiet stir of wings.

Hummingbird in the Book Store

Just browsing,
a hummingbird,
solo, on its way south,
flits into a book store,
examines dictionaries,
bestsellers, puzzles,
the latest fiction,
darts across a customer's
cap, lights in a hair-do,
investigates earrings,
wishing for flowers,
hoping for insects,
above all a shrub,
tries cookbooks,
greeting cards,
maps are useless,
flashes iridescence
as the cash-register ca-chings,
panics near the ceiling,
which is not the sky,
like all creatures,
yearns for light
and the path made clear.

Hummingbird

There.

She finally sees.
Hummingbird.

Male, nearly metallic red
reflective marking about its head
And then gone.

Her smile was a little bigger
and not the least bit forced.
Her eyes as bright as I could
remember.

"We have hummingbirds,"
She says.

"Yes,"
I nod squeezing her hand.

Genea Brice

Hummingbirds in C Sharp

    I hear ...
    ... strumming in the strings section ...
    ... humming coming from that direction ...

    Sheer flapping of tiny wings ...
    Clear clapping from shiny things ...
    ... Humming, yes, but she also sings ...
    ... because ... she knows ... the words ...

    ... As she hovers ...
    I am amazed
    At the ground she covers ...
    ... All the while, assuring her lovers ...
    ... that nectar awaits ...

James B. Nicola

Counterpoint

I sat up in a mysterious tree
and heard it say mysterious things
in perfect counterpoint — perfect but
for my being there with the audacity
to listen and breathe in perfection.
Twee and coo, then twee, then coo
and so on as if the tree had two mouths
which I'm sure it did — with mine, three.
But I remained silent, invisible to
the flush and green perfection.

Then there came a third voice
wee — ooo, wee — ooo,
accompanied so by the coo and the twee
in uncanny fugal harmony
that it grew even better for there being three
rather than just two.
And I realized it was a family tree
and that I was sitting in a world
as perfect as a world could be,
lacking you.

The cardinal and dove you might recognize
for their themes are as known as a lover's sighs;
the third was, I'll tell you, a chickadee;
the fourth, with only rests on the staff, me.
I'll sing when you get here and teach me a tune.
I hope it's soon.

David M. Harris

Dal Segno

    Birds abound along the river.
    I know the vireo by song if not by sight.
    I recognize the robin, jay, and mourning dove,
    not many more. I can tell a sparrow, but not which kind.
    My eyes on dog and path, my mind
    on Victoria's England. Jake runs ahead,
    chasing one more something, and an unhurried
    shape moves its slow shoulders and rises
    — and this I know, from all the icons and images —
    this eagle before me shrugs off the earth
    and lifts into apprehending flight.
    All pauses in that moment.
    Measured beats and a caesura,
    and then the other birds resume
    their rounds as though
    nothing has changed.

A New Tune

Every morning
the bird
outside my window
sings early,

much to my dismay.

But now
I wake
next to you,
and finally understand
his song.

Sylvia Ashby

Coasting

I would like to lie in your arms
sink into shelter
coast like a bird to a tree
bouyed by the air
till blanketed in green

Secure in their element
prevailing winds, extending hands
birds float into branches –
so confident, so certain
of a place to land.

Bird Got My Dreams

The morning after,
the night I got a parrot —
I found out that I talk in my sleep.

He said your name
over and over —
as I sipped
my tea.

I Kissed You with Sparrows

We are kissing each other on the lips
while hitting Love and wobbling around
only the walls are barricade to our lust.
Your mouth is beginning with a damp alphabet
a red butterfly settled on your face.

Look dear, sparrows are flapping in my rib cage.
I kissed you with sparrows from the thin places of your dreams.

Your breasts are two bunches of daisy
suddenly blooming through the sky of my mouth.
Then your breasts are a pensive river
flowing into the sea of my mouth.
I draw the purple map of lust on your skin by my mouth.

Look dear, sparrows are flapping in my rib cage.
I kissed you with sparrows from the thin places of your dreams.

Todd Cirillo

Homing Pigeons

Even from
this far away,
I hope
my message
finds you —

Baby,
come home —

you know
the way.

Homing

Nobody knows how pigeons
find their way home —
no kick of dust
or breadcrumbs littered,
not even the compass of guilt
or the smell of dumplings
frying on the stove.

They call it homing.

The ones who peck and bob
in Squares of Popes and Paupers
their bird brains whirring
their grey wings rising —

find their way.

But you and me
we close our eyes
our hands, not wings, reach up
and stick old pins on paper maps
unlike the bird
fear dust and eat the crumbs
of Christmas pies so long ago.
Unlike the bird, we future guess
north?
south?
east?
west?
anywhere, anywhere
but home.

Crusty

We've reached an understanding, he and I
sharing the same street corner
ignored by the same passersby.
His stained blanket mirrors my ragged wings
We both limp from hunger and on twisted limbs.
His fractured, fractious stories echo my plaintive call
His rheumy eyes, filth-clouded, reflect my skies, dismal.
We've both experienced the same fall from grace,
existing on life's edges in this wretched place.
He raids the bins, eats what he can, and what he can't he passes on.
When night crowds in, I rise to roost
watching over him till dawn.

Feeding the Birds in a Blizzard

Stranded in my house by the storm,
feeding oak and elm logs to the wood stove,
I feel secure as smoke rises from my chimney
and the chimneys of my rural neighbors.
Yet I worry about the pheasants
burrowing into snowdrifts for warmth,
the little chickadees and finches,
feathers flustered by the wind,
seeking shelter in woodpecker holes in dead trees,
the single robin doing the best it can,
competing with a gang of grackles
for the few crabapples left on the tree in my yard.

I worry about the people with nowhere to go
for shelter in this storm,
no one who cares enough to feed them.
Where will they go tonight,
with not even a stand of pine trees
to keep the wind at bay
and the storm predicted to intensify
when the dim light leaves the gray sky?

It would be foolish to drive into town in this weather,
the roads, drifted and unplowed,
impractical to gather the unsheltered from the sidewalks,
bring them home, offer them soup and a blanket,
a chair beside the fire in my hearth as the gospel bids us.
The best I can do today is the best I can do,
remember god is said to keep an eye on the sparrow, too,
so I shovel out the feeders again, refill them with seeds,
pray for everything else, myself included.

Annie Lighthart

The Safety of Birds

I thought of the safety of birds
though I had seen a dark goose
taken by a sudden eagle

Still afterwards
in that same sky
willing song

*

I thought of the safety of birds
though a dark body
was lifted

and flown low
into a far stand
of green trees

*

In my heart
is a green stand of trees

So much has disappeared there
and yet at a beautiful distance

its hunger moves
like green wind in the leaves

Mary Slocum

Safe

Ring-necked doves share my home, aviary large,
coo and sing, seldom try to escape.
Family, home and community draw them.
If they should leave,
they will meet me by the door the next day.
One escaped,
hawk pecked its eyes out sitting in the driveway.
I brought her home,
convenient water and food close by,
nursed her as best I could.
She lived two weeks – long enough
to tell the others not to go, tell her stories.
Hawk returned next year, killed and beheaded a dove
through the wire of aviary, in full view
of the community, safe on the other side of the cage.
When I came to feed them, the hawk waited close by, observing.
I knew she stayed for a reason, found her quarry, headless.
Placed it outside on a fence post
where she claimed it, left.
Now when I feed them, they light on my arm,
don't move when I reach for them.
Understand I'll keep them safe.
Other generations try less and less to get out.
They are home. I am a part of dove mother's stories now.

Safe is that place we all look for.
Safe is becoming harder to find.
Safe is not a metal box with a lock.
Safe is community.
Safe is home without the hawk.

White Feathers

    defiant on my patio
    we caught each other watching
    he sparred with my eyes

    but *el gavilán* did not blink
    the yellow of his look stayed firm
    like his feathers

    horrified I
          gasped and
    swallowed the soul
    of the dying dove
    in the clutch of his claws

    his ocher wings opened
    carrying away his prey

    white feathers swirled

    carrying away his prey
    his ocher wings opened

    in the clutch of his claws
    of the dying dove
    swallowed the soul
       gasped and
    horrified I

    like his feathers
    the yellow of his look stayed firm
    but *el gavilán* did not blink

    he sparred with my eyes

we caught each other watching
defiant on my patio

white feathers

Douglas Spangle

Wooden Eagles

Eagle River is named after eagles;
a couple of carved bald ones
flap sadly on the outskirts of town.
Every winter icicles dribble
down their painted beaks like snot.

One day she'd been driving
to work, she told me, when she saw
a real baldy, a monstrous thing
four feet tall or so,
tearing at rags of carrion,
monarch for a stretch of U.S. 51.

I do remember golden eagles
incising the sky when I was eight or nine,
in domains of aerial geometry,
treading so high that hot blue
brought tears when I looked up for them.

They stained those buff-colored cliffs
with rabbit shrieks and blood, but I
haven't seen eagles these eighteen years;
maybe there aren't any
more golden eagles or tears:

sinews frozen stiff with ice
and every artery hardened to wood.

Jack Little

Death by Cassowary

> *"The inner or second of the three toes is fitted with a long, straight, murderous nail which can sever an arm or eviscerate an abdomen with ease. There are many records of natives being killed by this bird…"*
>
> ~ *Ernest Thomas Gilliard (1958)*
> *Living Birds of the World*

Your campfire glimmers as you sup the final
dregs of beer from your can.
The thin, cold metal crunches between
your fingertips as you toss it aside.

Moonlight fills this area of forest.

You barely hear the gathering sound of crickets,
the crunching of leaves,
the gust of wind and the silence broken
by a deep cry howling from night.

Tiny frozen eyes merely observe.
The great blue bearded behemoth,
ancient Janus of the peacock
the bloodthirsty queen of this small place …

She asserts her dominance, arrogant and deadly.
You smash a fist of rock against its head
bludgeon her, she stumbles momentarily.

You measure her frozen stare
in units of fear and incredulity in equal measures,

A sharp pain scratches deep at your guts —

The moon hangs heavy overhead
blood trickles over the soil
your eyes slowly close, your last sensation
the stale taste of beer that remains on your tongue.

   *

Your eviscerated corpse is found some days later
with a note written by the cassowary in blood

   Ψ ... Ψ

Her territory has been marked.

Lucy Chau Lai-Tuen

China Is Not a Good Place to Be a Bird

Night sweeps in on the back of my hand
Car headlights target the rag-tag clusters
Li-men* jostling to sell you a live supper
Black-crowned night herons
Gaunt Egrets the sharp-eyed spinsters dressed for a better
place than this
White-breasted water hens dangle limply upside down
As if they have resigned themselves to their cooking pot fate
Side onto the road Li old, young and indifferent in age
Clutch onto bunches of legs attached to wild birds
Waving the birds in a roaring greeting to passersby
A stranger wanders over to the group inspecting the catch but
buying nothing
The older vendor with spit and spittle unleashes the words
"Ta kan ye bu mai!"
"He looks and doesn't even buy anything."
A violet thrush that whistles
Raising a beautiful eyebrow
The Hwamei with striking white eye makeup
The tropical cuckoo that lurks under thick cover
But breaks radio silence with a diphthong wolf-whistle
Sulphur crested cockatoos once the inmates of Flagstaff House
Fly in feral groups across Hong Kong air space
Loosed as the Japanese army came ever closer in 1941
What kind of Chinese bird am I?
Released in 1962 to fly in alien skies
Carrying my own murmuration of starlings
I long to be free screeching across the air
Like the feral cockatoos of Hong Kong.

*The early Chinese conquerors called the Li barbarians.
Modern Chinese still look down on the Li but hold them in high regard for their hunting skills.
This work was inspired by "The loneliness of the Chinese birdwatchers" by Zhoushan, 2008.

Duckling

Condos tower over a wetland sanctuary
      where painted turtles sun themselves on flat rocks
and
    dragonfly helicopters
        dart among the reeds
upon which red-winged blackbirds alight,
    swaying back and forth in the breeze;

damselflies skim the water
        looking for mosquito larvae and Daphnia,
    Canada Geese waddle imperiously along paths
next to the water
          glaring at passers-by

and mallard drakes submerge their emerald green heads
    searching for minnows and algae,
        their feathered bottoms bobbing upright
    above the water.

A female mallard glides along the surface of the pond
    leaving a triangular wake of ripples
        that jostles her already-imprinted brood
    of downy ducklings
          swimming to the shore

    where she starts to peck at the runt
  grabbing it by its nape with her bill
      and forcing its fuzzy head underwater
    again and again

despite the squawking of another female
    balancing diagonally on webbed feet
      flapping her wings in desperate protest

    against this infanticide —

an act so surreal
        that before it can even register
   in the minds of bystanders
            as more than spunky
maternal discipline,

the duckling floats
            limp
    on the water.

Grieving Mallards

The female mallard takes a fighter's stance
weaves and bobs
her quacks smack the air with body punches.
I'm the one you want,
me, I'm the one.
She lifts off, arcing away
from the grass-shrouded hillside,
the swoosh of her wings hiss her meaning
nothing
not one egg lies hidden
in the ferns dotting the uphill.

Two feathered rockets,
one dappled dun one teal glinted black
shoot toward the river, yank prying eyes
away from the eggs cached in knee high grass.
Both quack until their fear breaks the air.
Don't look don't look
where the eggs gleam alabaster.

Through green lattice the raccoon spies oval aglow.
With delicate fingers she pries open the shell
sucks and licks the orange globe, the clear pool.
The coyote doesn't need to look
he sniffs the air, the ground.
His jaws unhinge, his mouth plucks the egg —
one crunch the egg shatters,
one gulp he swallows.

They trudge up the hill.
The female's eyes shuttered,
her beak brushing the curve of the male's black tail feathers.
Her feet slap flat

mirror his steps as he traces slow S curves.
All is lost, all is lost,
the eggshells and the slime of life.
Only a slick shines in the hollowed-out nest.

Sharon Chmielarz

An Alignment in the Yard

A shingle-eater of a wind has blown
the robins' nest from its alcove
in an evergreen. The birds swarm
in a state above three blue eggs
crashed on the lawn.

It can't occur to two frantic natures
to use their beaks as hands to
grip each side of the nest and fly
their offspring back into the tree. Or,
maybe it does, but it doesn't work.

My sister at the window wonders why
God allows such things to happen,
confused perhaps by his love for lilies
of the field and the least sparrow, but absent
from the event she's watching in her yard.

I restrain a snarly comment. Why
upset her further? — Already she's out
on the lawn, finds one egg not cracked,
and lifts the nest back into place
though the two robins remain frantic,

wings all in a tizzy over the spot
where the world lost three robins,
and as of yesterday, when the female
spurned her mate's advances,
refuses a chance to begin again.

Alexa Mergen

Rock Dove

    The undersides of birds tell stories
    sweeps of wings won't reveal. See them,

    soft vessels of heart and blood above
    where you rest on your back in the hammock

    beneath the walnut tree. Remember
    holding a pigeon when you were small.

    White mites crawled among gray feathers
    as you stroked the bird with first and second

    fingers together, digits forming a paddle
    dipping into the dark lake of the bird's breast,

    holding with your other hand its heart, beating
    faster than your own, sluggish with afternoon

    heat, sweat dripping down the backs
    of your knees as you looked around the field

    behind the leased cottage for someone
    to take the bird and save it.

    You saw into the bird's red eye,
    the wrinkled membrane of its lid

    closed, and opened. You ran back
    to the white house with the slapping

    screen door, the bird held in front of you
    gently as a tray of china, to find a shoe box

and a jar lid of water. The ground feels
rougher when you're running barefoot

across a field to the fence-line of a summer house
bearing a life in need of saving.

John Grey

The Business of Caring

A bright red cardinal crashed against the window pane.
I held its stunned body for a moment in my palm.
A tiny heart beat softly until its eyes finally opened
and then that same organ shocked itself into overdrive.
My face looking down at it spurred it to panicked flight.
But I claimed the whole experience as a rescue.
Why not? On a regular basis, I attempt to ingratiate
myself into the lives of birds. I keep the outdoor
feeders as well stocked as a bar.
Would-be avian homes are scattered throughout the yard.
I fill the terra cotta bath so all feathered friends
can drink, cool off or splash as heartily as children.
Metal cages hang from trees, are stuffed with suet.
Woodpeckers come down out of the high branches to enjoy.
If I could, I'd wet-nurse their babies,
offer advice on avoiding hawks and neighborhood cats,
provide flight diagrams for fledglings,
operate a dating service for single birds.
A cardinal needing my attention is a 911 call
on the one hand but a breath of fresh air on the other.
It needs protection from predators.
And I am more than willing to provide that protection.
It's not my fault that it takes to the sky without
a trill of gratitude. I walk back into the house,
feeling as relieved but proud as the ER must
after resuscitating a patient. My wife plans to sticker
that window with decals so birds will no longer mistake
it for air space. Good for her. Meanwhile, the weather's
turning colder. I wonder how the spiders in the shed are faring.

Brown Duck

In the latest evening,
an unremarkable brown duck returns
from a night foraging,
expecting to find her eggs just as she left them.

Taken to ground, she settles upon her nest,
hardly to blink for all the next day.
She'll never think about the man
who rushed from his house in a hailstorm
to cover her roost with a window-well protector
until danger had ebbed away.

Days later, as she fidgets and squirms,
trying to keep her hatchlings safe
beneath her for a few hours more,
the man is pleased.

And when she leads her young to the river,
she has no time for good-byes or thank-yous,
cannot consider miracles or moments of transcendence —

or what hope means to a human being
and how thankful we are for it
even when there is no one left to thank.

Bird I Never Saw in Daylight

It hit the windshield, changed parabola
of flight.   You braked the car,
ran back.
         Great horned owl broken
in the ditch. Quite dead.

How gently you cradled it
to the trunk. How many lambs like ours

disappeared to its talons.
                Such a beauty.
You folded it in plastic,
to ship to the museum.

    Now our windshield
begins its fine-calligraphy fault-
         line, a glass

trajectory of dawn-dim into bright.
         Inside the Hall of Ornithology

         Owl stares down
from its beaked   mask,
         fixed forever-eyes, its voided
breast and fluted bones
              immobilized in flight.

Elegy

    Little robin, with fiery
    breast nestled atop
    the burning leaves of autumn.
    Your belly is a carved pumpkin.

    Your fractured wings are
    tipped with frost,
    neck craned at a
    peculiar angle as if
    searching for some
    pattern in the clouds
    or in the world.

    A tiny sliver of pink tongue
    slips out of your open
    mouth, and stiff
    skeletal limbs reach
    toward the heights you'll never
    again achieve.

    You,
    dead plaything of curious
    school boys, can only hope
    that some child (maybe five
    or six years old) will
    wrap your hollow body
    in her favorite blue scarf and
    quite ceremoniously
    plant you between rows of
    withered brown weeds
    in her mother's flower garden.
    And mourn.

Matilda Died Today

She flew squawking from the kitchen
to land on my shoulder. She brought me
the tiny burden of her death.
I caught her up, hugged her to me
as if I could hold it off;
I breathed into her lungs,
pumped her wings, I couldn't see –
my tears blinded me –
but she wouldn't come back. I held
her limp body, neck swinging loose
as if broken, feathers disarrayed
as she would never have them, eyes
shuttered, then closed.
Slowly she got cold.

This morning when she'd hopped
onto my hand, I'd noticed
her feet were cool. Usually
she's warm.

Now she's buried, wrapped
in a pink silk chemise of mine,
under the pohutukawa near the tui's nest
and a blackbird is singing
her tangihanga.

I'm putting away her things. I need
to list them before she's gone altogether.

First, I put her seed dish outside
for the sparrows and finches, blackbirds
who'll miss her daily leftovers. I'll fill it

every day until the bags of seed
run out.

Her water bowl will rejoin
odd garden stuff. She'd floated
one of her toys — the bowl
of an old wooden spoon —
in it this morning.
I don't know why.

Her swing
with a concrete perch to help
trim her claws, her mirror with dangling bell
that never chimed, just clunked,
the boiled lamb bone for her beak,
the cuttlefish, the shell grit — all into the garbage
with the half-explored apricot, the sampled
but not finished apple, the eggplant end,
the cabbage bone, lettuce leaf, and the chewed
and splintered wooden spoon handle, the honey
dripper with its grooves neatly rounded.
Her spirit is still imprinted in them
but it's fading. A fly
just landed on the cage bottom.

Now I bend and fold the sprig of leaves
from the big gum on the corner by Ian's house
near the railway lines — it still has a few
gum nuts on it, not yet chewed.
She smelled of eucalyptus when I breathed her in
just before I put her in the ground
and covered her
just an hour ago, just this morning.

Her ladder — she was scared of it at first
but climbing the cage walls hurt her feet
and the ladder made it easier. I put it

where she's buried, leading up into the sky.

I throw away her other mirror, that I'd taken
from my mother's nursing home — a folding
double vanity mirror I'd hooked to the cage
with a key ring from Las Vegas.

Matilda died this morning. Already in the past.

Last things — that flower John brought her
from Porirua, whose name I still don't know.
It grew at his place. Tuis and kakas loved it too,
he shared it with Matilda for months;
it had just finished flowering, these were
the last stems.

A wilted fag-end of a carrot. The newspaper
dated December 4. A dried-up locquat
and a few feathers. She'd finished her molt
just in time to die

and the pink-and-grey rose-covered comforter
I'd bought new when Mum was still alive
that had covered her cage every night
that I lifted every morning
to let the world back in.

I won't need that again.

'the tiny burden of her death' from "*Death of the Bird*" by A D Hope.

Maureen O'Brien

The Birds She Never Asked For

Every night she dreams of dead birds in her hands
dreams of their tranquil faces and jade wings
she must scoop the birds into her bare hands
to bury them in her palms
every night she cradles a new bird
until it disappears

weeks have passed and months
each night a bird dies and she does what a mother must do
she cups
the last flutter
months have passed and now a year and still
she is terrified that she will never understand
what the birds are trying so hard to tell her

Irene Bloom

Empty Nester

With long tapered bill
the female flicker drums
out a woodland song –
her new claim on the hollow trunk
soon to house a new noisy clutch
klee you - klee you she calls.

Can she recall her fledglings
who flew at only four weeks?
Does she feel a longing to see them?
Will their black scalloped plumes
that fall to the forest floor remind
her of the loss?

In another tree a house wren remodels
downy feathers, slivers of grass
and silky spider egg sacs
line her abode.
She too will nurture her
helpless and naked nestlings
Protect the brood from constant predator,
squirrel and snake, rat and raccoon
For them she will fret and flit,
forage and churr.

Perhaps in another life
I shall return as a mourning dove –
devoted mother who sings to
her squabs and holds them close
Perhaps the forest will ring
with a requiem of sadness
the *coo coo cooing* for the young
when they have gone

 Christopher Leibow

The Coffin Maker

He sits in small room making coffins
for birds, reads operas,
Searches the sky
for the initial fall.

He follows goats
up impossible
inclines
at the summit
he fills the tiny
spaces with stolen sky
binds it with laquers, nails it
to the sides of tiny boxes.

Walks derilect parks
with nets, the hollowed
out bodies of bird
freed from the weight
of soul begin to ascend.

He ties brass weights
around legs and gathers
a reaping of flight.

In his room
the birds float
like feathered balloons
He takes each body
washes it gently with
holy water stolen
from a winged cistern.

Wraps them in blue shrouds

fragmented clouds stiched
to cloth. Lays the body in
the small coffin and the tiny
sky.

Seals each lid with wax.
He collects three
coffins, walks the flight
of stairs.

On the roof, he ties the
coffins down, they knock in
the wind like wood
dirigibles.

He wears a prayer shawl,
hums Mahler's 9th.

Each coffin is then
set free, floating like
a feather on a thermal
higher, higher
then like Icarus
the wax melts.

Heaven receiving the body,
Earth
a shattered box
of sky.

Hot Twelve O'clock

Biggest and baldest of eagles clutches a lunch
of seagull, screams ugly, muscles up
her black wings in a high V, the mirrored
white chevron hang-gliding from her talons.

Hot twelve o'clock allows itself to be fondled,
consoled, by a big cool gust, which has just
blown in through the doors and snatched
from the dining table what had been

a short stack of torn magazine pages –
poems too good to read once and let go –
and transformed it into a small flock
of gleaming dead gulls falling from thermals.

What bird, balcony, branch will catch the black
words on white paper: *Running Scared,*
The Dog's Tooth, Summer Grace,
What I Did With Your Ashes?

Jane Yolen

The Sorrowing of Birds

When I think of you,
I hear birds soaring,
sorrowing above the trees,
their songs, perfect phrases of grief,
where once I heard joy.

The tapping of woodpeckers
I decode into elegies,
The peeping of hatchlings
under the bathroom window
are constant spring reminders
of my loss.

How can I let it go entire,
when the birds are my memory,
when every morning they sing
an oratorio to their old friend.
There is finality in obituary,
but not true closure,
even eight years along.

Bird song and its soaring sorrow
sustains me even
while it makes me linger
longer in the past.
I need no recordings of birdsong
to remind me,
just the open window
and the dawn.

Dianne Avey

Impossible Ledges

Black crow pecking at my ankles all day,
tap, tap, tap – Poe's Raven?
Envoy of grief, the unwelcome ambassador of your death.
Obsidian beak tearing away
bits of my flesh, no one notices his work
I'm weary of this visitor.
Driving home, I can barely stand the beat
of the windshield wipers, thud-screech-thud-screech.

I decide to take the long way home,
through slick city streets where tight roads
hem me in with distraction. But even here,
the raven scavenges its evening meal, pestering
delicate sparrows that nest on impossible ledges,
and tramples soft ferns that find their way
through crevices in the night sidewalks.

Maybe tomorrow, I'll drive home past
the wide open field, braving the marsh filled
with late Autumn light. Where rosehips hang
like ruby baubles, and the air is clear and waiting
for me to stop, long enough to remember
that elusive full breath.
The one that goes all the way
down to my belly. The breath that I haven't known
since you've left.

Yes, maybe tomorrow I'll stop there. I'll sit on the bank,
dangle my bruised ankles in the cool water.
There, where the red tail spirals high,
the heron patiently waits, and
even the crows are silent.

His World

My brother was always talking birds
gannets, fulmars, shags,
pointing out the tell-tale white flash
of the wheatear; the red beak and legs of choughs,
their distinctive call.
A kestrel anchored to the sky.
Once he convinced me to lie for hours in the harsh
marram grass, waiting for Manx Shearwaters
to stream in, bodies skimming the ocean
stiff black wings blotting out light.
There was always a pair of glasses round his neck
or resting on the dashboard.

Although I loved him
I envied his freedom
that male prerogative to wander at will
on nothing more than the rumour
of a stork blown off-course.

Like Icarus he flew too close to the sun,
died before his time.
When the funeral mass was over
I asked for his binoculars.
For months they sat on the sideboard.
When at last I raised them to my eyes
all I could see was a blur.

Phoenix

I was born with a cockscomb;
A flash of black
Across the dome of my head.

I was raised with knowledge;
A flash of faculty
I would emit over time.

I never perceived
A nimbus around my presence;
A halo, glowing
On my golden, crimson wings.

Inside I was afire,
With a turbulent flame.
Flying through the darkened forest,
I never planned to bring forth
The Inferno, but
The complexity of ancient oaks,
Illuminated with the rays.

I was ensnared in a cage of dogma;
Symbol of power
That yoked my flight.

I was strangled by autocratic hand;
Symbol of silence
That yoked my verse.

Inside I was afire,
With a turbulent flame.
My feathers falling from me,
To those who knew

Heaven and its beauty and
The complexity of faint hopes
Illuminated with the rays.

And from the chaos of my ashes,
I rose into the firmament.
I was the phoenix again,
Billowed by freedom's fair wind.

Inside I was afire,
With a turbulent flame.
Pearls cast out of my beak,
Like a trace, trailing to
Eternity and its potential; the
Complexity of my hundred-song,
Illuminated by the rays.

Behind the Mountains

I saw the birds in their free flight,
And in my dreams I fly with them.
Over cages of wild beasts and beings.
Through clouds of smoke and ash.
Ash of bones and flesh.
Dry leaves and cracked streets.
They fly into darkness,
behind the mountains.

Arrangements

After satin-lined casket
or ashes in the urn
after the tears —
maybe some kind of procession —
family and friends gathered
for stories and beer.

Those are details for the living.
I ask just one favor.

Could you find one
Great Blue Heron
living the sky
with her feet in the water

measured wing-falls to carry
my soul to the next world.

Acknowledgments

We gratefully acknowledge the following publications in which these poems first appeared:

"BirdBath" by Elizabeth Reninger was published in *And Now The Story Lives Inside You* (Woven Word Press, 2005)

"Decoding Sparrows" by Mariano Zaro appeared under the title "My Father's Biology Lesson" in *Levure Littéraire* (Issue No. 9)

"Finding Compass" by Carolyn Martin was previously published in *Finding Compass* (Queen of Wands Press, 2011)

A version of "The Hajj of Canada Geese" by Parker Bauman appeared in *Earthen Lamp Journal* (November, 2014)

"Hope Between Chaos" by Stephen Linsteadt was published previously in *Cadence Collective: Long Beach Poets* (Jan 3, 2015)

"Ornithology" by Connie Post first appeared in *I-70 Review* (Summer/Fall, 2014)

"The Language of Birds" by Linda Strever was published in *CALYX: A Journal of Art and Literature by Women* (Volume 26, Number 2, Winter, 2011)

"Red Shoes" by Tricia Knoll first appeared in *Urban Wild* (Finishing Line Press, 2014)

"Well Hidden" by M.J. Iuppa was first published by *The Victorian Violet Press Journal* and reprinted in *Little Eagle's Re/Verse*

"Owls" by Davnet Heery first appeared in *Ropes Anthology* (Spring, 2014)

"Bird Bones" by Marybeth Rua-Larsen was first published by the Wickford Art Association in *Poetry and Art: an exhibition of contemporary art and responsive poetry* (July, 2014)

"Scarecrow" by Pete Mullineaux first appeared in *Session* (Salmon Poetry, 2011)

"The Crows' Field" by Michael Shay was previously published in *The Cape Rock* (Vol. 38, No. 1, 2008)

"What They See" by Shawn Aveningo first appeared as "Bird-Watching" in *Songs of Eretz Poetry Review* (March, 2015)

"Birds as Omens for a Change" by M previously appeared in *Poems Niederngasse* (October, 2000) and *To That Mythic Country Called Closure* (Concrete Wolf Press, 2013)

"Little Bombardiers" by Marie Lecrivain was first published in *Kentucky Review* (Issue One, 2014)

"Birds Over Mainframes" by Arturo Desimone first appeared in *African Writing Magazine* (Issue 12)

"Pigeons" by Cynthia Gallaher was published in *Earth Elegance* (March Abrazo Press, Chicago)

"Birds" by Lytton Bell was previously published in *Cyclamens and Swords* (August, 2013)

"Dal Segno" by David M. Harris first appeared in *The Rearview Mirror* (Unsolicited Press, 2013)

"I Kissed You with Sparrows" by Serkan Engin was first published in *Empty Mirror Literary & Arts Magazine* (2014)

"The Safety of Birds" by Annie Lighthart was published in *Iron String* (Airlie Press, 2013)

"Wooden Eagles" by Douglas Spangle was published in *A White Concrete Day, poems: 1978-2013* (Reprobate/GOBQ Books, 2013)

"Rock Dove" by Alexa Mergen was previously published in *The Redwood Coast Review*

"Brown Duck" by Richard King Perkins II was originally published in *Broad River Review* (Spring, 2014)

"Bird I Never Saw in Daylight" by Taylor Graham first appeared in *Jellyfish Whispers* (July 16, 2014)

"The Birds She Never Asked For" by Maureen O'Brien was first published in *The Other Cradling* (Finishing Line Press, 2011)

"Hot Twelve O'clock" by Lillo Way was originally published in *Poetry East*

"Phoenix" by Marcas Mac an Tuairneir has been published previously in Gaelic as "Ainneamhag" in *The Grind* and also won the 2014 Baker Prize for Gaelic Writing in the *Isle of Skye*

Contributors

Alexa Mergen's teaches yoga in Washington, DC and leads movement-based poetry workshops throughout the United States. Her most recent chapbook is *Winter Garden* (Meridian, 2015). Please visit Yoga Stanza for a full list of publications and upcoming events. Alexa loves to walk in the rain, day or night. Her favorite bird is the Mountain Bluebird. <yogastanza.org>

Alisa Golden writes, makes art, and teaches bookmaking at California College of the Arts in Oakland. Most days she takes photos of objects she finds on the sidewalk; some days she writes, draws, paints, or makes felt. Her stories, poems, and essays have been published in several magazines including *100 Word Story*, *The Monthly*, and *NANO Fiction*, among others. She is the author of *Making Handmade Books* and the editor of *Star 82 Review*. Alisa's favorite bird is the Phoebe. <neverbook.com>

Allegra Silberstein grew up on a farm in Wisconsin but has lived in California since 1963. Her love of poetry began as a child when her mother would recite poems as she worked. In addition to three chapbooks of poetry, she is widely published in journals and a growing number on-line. In March, 2010, Allegra became the first Poet Laureate for the city of Davis, California and served until September 2012. She is also a dancer with the Third Stage dance company and sings and plays washboard with Front Porch Bluegrass in Davis. Allegra's favorite birds are Robins and the Oregon Junco.

Annie Lighthart started writing poetry after her first visit to an Oregon old-growth forest. Since those first strange days, she published her poetry collection *Iron String* with Oregon's Airlie Press and earned an MFA in Poetry from Vermont College. Annie has taught at Boston College, as a poet in the schools, and now teaches workshops through Mountain Writers. She lives in a small green corner of Portland. Annie's favorite bird is the Penguin. <annielighthart.com>

Ariana Kramer has been writing poetry for most of her life. While living in Portland, Oregon, she earned degrees in Biology and Education for Leadership in Ecology, Culture and Learning. She is inspired by the natural world, and people's relationship to it and one another. Currently living in her hometown of Taos, New Mexico, Ariana works as a freelance writer and writes for *The Taos News*, covering music and the arts. <arianakramer@hotmail.com>

Arturo Desimone is an Argentinean citizen born and raised on the island Aruba in the Dutch Caribbean. At the age of 23 he emigrated to the Netherlands, but after six years, he decidedly embarked on a nomadic life-style that proved more conducive to writing poetry and brought him to live in such places as (post)-revolutionary Tunisia. He is currently based between the Netherlands and Buenos Aires Argentina. His poems and short fiction pieces have appeared in journals, like *New Orleans Review*, *Acentos Review*, *Counterpunch Poets Basement*, *The Original Van Gogh's Ear Poetry Series* and *Hamilton Stone*. His favorite birds are the Bananaquit and the Chuchubi.

Beth MacFarlane, a jack of all trades, master of some, finds happiness in making things. Now in her 5th decade she has turned her creative energy towards words. Her work has appeared in *Abridged Literary Journal*, and *Torrid Literature Journal*. Her love of birds has appeared in all aspects of her life. Beth lives in Montclair, NJ where she always keeps an eye to the sky. Her favorite bird is the Belted Kingfisher.

Bobbi Sinha-Morey is a poet living in the peaceful city of Brookings, Oregon. Her poetry can be seen in places such as *Orbis*, *Plainsongs*, *Gloom Cupboard*, *The Path*, and *Carillon*, among others. Her books of poetry are available on Amazon.com and www.writewordsinc.com. She loves aerobics and knitting, and her favorite bird is the Lovebird.

Brenda Taulbee lives, loves, and writes from Portland, Oregon. Her work has been published by several local, international, and online publications including *The Inflectionist Review*, *The Gobshite Quarterly*, and *Keeping It Weird*. You can find the chronicle of her frequently ridiculous life and times in her blog, *b Honest*, with her editor, Murphy the cat's, seal of approval. Her favorite bird is the Blue Heron. <honest-b.blogspot.com>

Brigit Truex has left the Sierra foothills after a dozen years for the rolling fields of bluegrass in Lexington KY. During that time, she produced numerous poems, on such topics as current events, water and wildlife. Her work has appeared in various journals including *Tule Review*, *Atlanta Review*, *Canary*, *Yellow Medicine Review* and others. She was a featured poet at Verse on the Vine® as well as many of the Red Fox Poetry Underground readings. Her latest book is *Strong as Silk* (Lummox Press).

Carolyn Martin is blissfully retired in Clackamas, OR, where she gardens, writes and plays with creative colleagues. Her poems have appeared in publications such as *Stirring*, *Persimmon Tree*, *Antiphon* and *Naugatuck River Review*. Her second collection, *The Way a Woman Knows*, was released in February, 2015 by The Poetry Box®. Her favorite bird is the Ring-Tailed Parrot. <TheWayaWomanKnows.com>

Catherine Ayres is a teacher, living and working in Northumberland, England. Her poems have appeared in *Ink, Sweat and Tears, Spontaneity, Domestic Cherry, StepAway, Prole* and *The Moth*. She recently came third in *Ambit* magazine's "Under the Influence" competition. Catherine often sits on her bed and watches the pigeons and jackdaws in the cul de sac behind her house. It's significantly better entertainment than TV. Her favorite bird is the Oystercatcher.

Chris Jarmick is a sporadically published writer/poet (*Seattle Weekly, Pontoon, Cambridge Book Review, Military Times, Rattle, Raven Chronicles* and others) who has hosted and curated regularly scheduled readings, events and open mics since 2001. His latest poetry collection *Ignition: Poem Starters...* was published in 2010 and his next, *Not Aloud*, is due out in September of 2015 from MoonPath Press. <chrisjarmick.wordpress.com>

Christa Kaainoa is a writer, rock climber, feminist, activist, life enthusiast, middle school English teacher, and mother of three living in Portland, Oregon. Her poetry has been featured in *VoiceCatcher: a journal of women's voices and visions*. Christa's favorite bird is the Crow.

Christopher Leibow is an internationally obscure poet, a visual artist and a performer of small slights of hand. He is an MFA graduate of Antioch and has been published in numerous journals and online, including *Vayavya, the Moth, Nano, 2 Bridges* and the *Sugarhouse Review*. He is a two time Pushcart Award nominee and a Utah Book Award Nominee and the winner of the *Writers@Work* Writers Advocate Award in 2008. He currently lives in the burbs with his wife, newborn son and dog Miss Penelope the Perpetual Wonder Pup.

Claire T. Feild has had 325 poems accepted for publication in 106 print journals and anthologies such as *The Tulane Review; Pinyon Review; Windmills* (Australia); *Coup d'Etat; San Pedro River Review; Vine Leaves Literary Journal* (Greece); and *The Carolina Quarterly*. Her first poetry book is *Mississippi Delta Women in Prism*. Her second book (non-fiction), is *A Delta Vigil: Yazoo City*, Mississippi, the 1950s. Claire's favorite bird is the Hummingbird.

Connie Post served as Poet Laureate of Livermore, California (2005 to 2009). Her work has appeared in *Calyx, Kalliope, Crab Creek Review, Comstock Review, Spoon River Poetry Review* and others. She won the 2009 Caesura Poetry Award & the Dirty Napkin Cover Prize. Her chapbook *And When the Sun Drops* won the Aurorean Fall 2012 Editors Choice award. Her First full length collection *Floodwater* (Glass Lyre Press) won the Lyrebird Award in 2014.

Cynthia Gallaher, a Chicago-based poet, playwright and nonfiction writer, is author of three full poetry collections and a writing workshop leader. She is on the Chicago Public Library's list of "Top Ten Requested Chicago Poets." Her most recent chapbook is *Omnivore Odes: Poems About Food, Herbs and Spices*. Follow her on Twitter @swimmerpoet.

Darren Donohue is a poet and playwright from Co. Kilkenny, Ireland. He was shortlisted for the Desmond O'Grady Poetry Prize, 2012 and a Hennessy Literary Award in 2012 & 2014. His short poetry collection "The Pinch", was Highly Commended by Munster Literary Pamphlet Competition, 2014. Darren's poems are also published in a number of leading European literary journals. He is currently putting the finishing touches to his first collection. Darren's favorite bird is the Robin Redbreast.

David Butler is a multi-award-winning writer from Ireland with three novels, a short story collection, a poetry collection and a play in print to date. The poetry collection, *Via Crucis*, was published by Doghouse in 2011; poems included in it such as 'Swallows', 'Magpies' and 'Pheasant Plucker' already give an intimation of an unhealthy ornithological bent.

Until 2003, **David M. Harris** had never lived more than fifty miles from New York City. Since then he has moved to Tennessee, married, acquired a daughter and a classic MG, and gotten serious about poetry. All these projects seem to be working out pretty well. His work has appeared in *Pirene's Fountain, Gargoyle, The Labletter, The Pedestal*, and other places. His first collection of poetry, *The Review Mirror*, was published by Unsolicited Press (Sept, 2013). His favorite bird is the Cardinal.

Davnet Heery hails from Connemara on the west coast of Ireland, where she lives close by the shore, and is frequently found chatting with seals. She is the 2012 winner of The McLlelan poetry prize. Published in Cyphers, The Stony Thursday Book, Hennessy New Irish Writing, Galway Review, Ropes etc., she is a graduate of the MA in Writing from NUIG. Her favorite bird is the Wren.

Deborah Meltvedt is a Medical Science and Creative Writing high school teacher. She has been published in the Sacramento literary journals that include the *Tule Review, The American River Literary Review*, Sacramento City College's *Susurrus Review* and the true story anthology *Under the Gum Tree*. Deborah also received an Honorable Mention in fiction for *Glimmer Train*. Deborah lives with her writer husband, Rick Kushman and their cat, Anchovy Jack, who used to be a pirate. Her favorite bird is the Blue-Footed Booby.

Dianne Avey lives in the Northwest where she is a fifth generation islander on Anderson Island. She shares a seaside home with her new husband, her son, and two lazy dogs. She writes poetry when she can, often on the ferry while commuting to her job as a Nurse Practitioner. She is published in *Wrist Magazine*, *Sibella*, *Pulse* and in *Something's Brewing*. She is working on a collection of poems of grief and recovery following the loss of her husband to leukemia in 2006. Dianne's favorite birds are Red-Tailed Hawks and American Goldfinches.

Donna McLaughlin Schwender's work has appeared in Grey Wolfe Publishing's *Legends*, Haunted Waters Press' *From the Depths*, Prompt and Circumstance's *Promptly*, and Raging Aardvark Publishing's *Twisted Tales*. Once upon a time, Donna was a Wildlife Biologist for the U.S. Fish and Wildlife Service. Now she's a self-professed word nerd, feather finder, heart stone hunter, and synchronicity searcher whose favorite birds are Ravens and Crows. <heartstonefeathers.com>

Doug Draime's most recent full-length book is *More Than The Alley* (Interior Noise Press, 2012). Also, available are chapbooks: *Dusk With Carol* (Kendra Steiner Editions), *Los Angeles Terminal: Poems 1971-1980* (Covert Press), *In Back of Madam Wong's* (Tree Killer/Epic Rites Press), and an online chap, *Speed of Light* (Right Hand Pointing). He's been awarded PEN grants and nominated for several Pushcart Prizes. A presence in the literary 'underground' since the late 1960's, he currently lives in the foothills of the Cascade mountain range on the outskirts of Medford, Oregon. His favorite bird is the Raven.

Douglas Spangle has lived all over the West, in the Mideast and Europe. He came to Portland in 1978 and stuck around, busy on the local literary scene. In 2015, he was nominated for Pushcart, Hazel Hall and Stewart Holbrook Awards for his poem "The Birches," his collection *A White Concrete Day, poems: 1978-2013* (Reprobate/GobQ Books) and his general literary service. He lives with his wife Christine on the sunny slopes of Mt. Tabor, perhaps the world's only urban volcano.

Eileen McGurn is, among other things, a teacher and a poet. She has published both on the East Coast (where she's from) and the West Coast (where she now, happily, lives). She currently works at the PACE Program for pregnant and parenting students in the North Clackamas School District. There, she teaches Language Arts, Social Studies, Creative Writing and anything else that needs teaching (except Math) to the most wonderful students in the world. Her poem "Crows and Keys" is one section of a larger work-in-progress on her favorite bird, the Crow. <mcgurne@nclack.k12.or.us>

Elizabeth Reninger writes poetry, teaches yoga and qigong, has tea with friends and enjoys the mountains in Boulder, Colorado. She holds an M.S. in Chinese medicine, and continues to be inspired by the deep wisdom of Taoism, Buddhism and Advaita Vedanta. She is the author of a collection of poems *And Now The Story Lives Inside You* (Woven Word Press, 2005) and *Meditation Now – A Beginner's Guide* (Althea Press, 2015). Elizabeth's favorite bird is the Swan. <halfmoon108@yahoo.com>

Following retirement from Kansas University's English Department, where she was known as a Melville scholar, **Elizabeth Schultz** became a dedicated advocate for the arts and the environment. She continues to write about the people and places she loves and has published two scholarly books, five books of poetry, a memoir, a collection of short stories, and a collection of essays. Her scholarly and creative work has appeared in numerous journals and reviews. Her favorite bird is the Belted Kingfisher. <eschultz@ku.edu>

Fern G. Z. Carr is a former lawyer, teacher and president of the Society for the Prevention of Cruelty to Animals. A member of the League of Canadian Poets and 2013 Pushcart Prize nominee, she composes and translates poetry in five languages. Carr has been published extensively from Finland to the Seychelles, has had her work recognized by the Parliamentary Poet Laureate and currently has one of her poems orbiting the planet Mars aboard NASA'S MAVEN spacecraft. Her favorite bird is the Saw-Whet Owl. <ferngzcarr.com>

Fred Zirm is a recently retired English and drama teacher with a B.A. and M.A. in English from Michigan State and an M.F.A. in playwriting from the University of Iowa. His poetry and flash fiction have been published in *Voices de la Luna*, *Still Crazy*, *The Rejected Quarterly*, *Red Wolf Journal*, *Silver Birch Press*, *The Rainbow Journal*, *Form Quarterly*, and *NEAT*. He lives in Rockville, MD and is also an avid cyclist who has scaled many of the major climbs of the Tour de France. Fred's favorite bird is the Nuthatch. <poetry181.blogspot.com>

G. Murray Thomas has been an active part of the SoCal poetry scene for over 20 years. He has performed throughout the L.A. area and beyond. His most recent book of poetry is *My Kidney Just Arrived* (Tebot Bach, 2011). His previous books are *Cows on the Freeway* and *Paper Shredders*, an anthology of surf writing. He has also published five chapbooks, and has been widely published in various literary magazines. His parents are avid birders, and is favorite bird is the Scarlet Macaw. <gmurraythomas.com>

Gary Beck spent most of his life as a theater director. He has 11 published chapbooks & poetry collections include: *Days of Destruction* (Skive Press),

Expectations (Rogue Scholars Press). *Dawn in Cities, Assault on Nature, Songs of a Clerk, Civilized Ways*, with *Perceptions and Displays* accepted (Winter Goose Publishing). Novels include: *Extreme Change* (Cogwheel Press) *Acts of Defiance* (Artema Press). *Flawed Connections* accepted for publication (Black Rose Writing). His short story collection, *A Glimpse of Youth* (Sweatshoppe Publications). His favorite bird is the Downy Woodpecker.

Poet, author, and teacher, **Genea Brice** resides in Vallejo, California. After earning her BA and Master's Degrees, she became a classroom teacher and dabbled in local politics. Genea's poetry can be found in *The Colors of Life* (2003), *The Best Poems and Poets of 2005, A Word for All Seasons* (2014), and is the author of an autobiographical work: *Weaned in the Desert: Souvenirs from Sacred Seasons with my Savior*. Her favorite bird is the Hummingbird.

Georgette Howington is a naturalist, horticulturist, gardener and writer whose niche is Backyard Habitat and secondary-cavity nesters. She is a County Coordinator and Assistant State Program Director for the California Bluebird Recovery Program. Georgette has had articles on gardening and conservation subjects published and most recently, poetry.

Gerald Yelle teaches high school English in Greenfield, MA – so he knows the meaning of work. His poems have appeared in print and online. *The Holyoke Diaries* is his first published collection. A second, *Mark My Word and the New World Order* is scheduled to be published by The Pedestrian Press. He is a member of the Florence (MA) Poets Society. His favorite bird is the Crow. <geraldyelle.blogspot.com>

Hannah Kate Elliott Heltsley (9/14/1982 – 11/15/2014). She loved Seattle, the green growing things, water, ferries, and fish flingers at the Pike Place Market. Her friends, old and new, are remembering her kindness, humor, infectious smile and the splendor and expense of fragility. You will be missed, Weeblet. May your journey be swift, sure and full of peace.

Irene Bloom is an emerging poet from Seattle, Washington. Her work has appeared in *Poetry Super Highway* and *Drash Northwest Mosaic*. She received an honorable mention for her poem "The Carrier" in the Reuben Rose Poetry Competition, published in the 2014 *Voices Israel* Anthology. She also published a chapbook collection entitled *Stirrings*. Much of Irene's poetry is inspired by her world travels, love of language and of course, fondness of birds.

Jack Little (b. 1987) is a British poet, translator and editor based in Mexico City. He is the founder of The Ofi Press and his work has most recently been published in *Wasafiri, Under the Radar* and *The Screech Owl*. His first pamphlet will be published by Eyewear Press in autumn 2015. Jack is a former international cricketer with the Mexican national team. His favorite bird is the Hummingbird. <ofipress.com>

Widely published in periodicals including *The Southwest, Atlanta, Lullwater* and *Texas Reviews,* **James B. Nicola** has several poetry awards and nominations to his credit. His nonfiction book *Playing the Audience* won a *Choice* award. A Yale grad and also a stage director, composer, lyricist, and playwright, his children's musical *Chimes: A Christmas Vaudeville* premiered in Fairbanks, Alaska, where Santa Claus was in attendance on opening night. His favorite bird is the Cardinal. <sites.google.com/site/jamesbnicola>

Jane Yolen, called the Hans Christian Andersen of America by *Newsweek* in a surfeit of enthusiasm, is the author of over 350 books, mostly for children. *Owl Moon* (Caldecott Medal winner) is about her birder husband taking their daughter owling. She has eight books of adult poetry and over 70 books of poetry for young readers and been named Grand Master of SFPA, the Science Fiction/Fantasy Poetry Assn. Six colleges and universities have given her honorary doctorates. Jane's favorite bird is the Great Horned Owl.

Jennifer Kemnitz is an herbalist and amateur astrologer who writes from the edge of Portland. Her work has been anthologized by *Poetry on the Lake* and *VoiceCatcher* and is forthcoming from *We'Moon*. Jennifer's favorite bird is the Varied Thrush. <ereshkigal54@hotmail.com>

Joan Colby has published 16 books and chapbooks, the most recent of which include *The Wingback Chair* (FutureCycle Press), *Ah Clio* (Kattywompus Press) and *Pro Forma* (Foothills Publishing). Her work has appeared in journals such as *Poetry, Atlanta Review, South Dakota Review* and others. Her favorite bird is the Crow.

Joan Leotta has been playing with words with writing and performing since childhood. Her 'motto' is "encouraging words through pen and performance." Her award-winning poetry, short stories, books and articles have appeared in many journals, magazines and newspapers. She performs folklore and one-woman shows on historic figures in schools libraries, museums and at festivals. Joan lives in Calabash, NC with husband Joe. Her favorite birds include Egrets, Cardinals, Sparrows and Blue Jays. <joanleotta.wordpress.com>

John Grey is an Australian born poet. Recently published in *Paterson Literary Review, Rockhurst Review* and *Spindrift* with work upcoming in *New Plains Review,*

Leading Edge and *Louisiana Literature*. John's favorite birds are Cockatoos and Chickadees.

John Saunders' first collection *After the Accident* was published in 2010. His poems have appeared in many poetry journals in Ireland, The United Kingdom and America and in numerous online journals. His second collection *Chance* was published in April 2013 by New Binary Press.

Judy Darley is a British poet, fiction writer and journalist. Recent publications include poetry, flashes and short stories in *Streetcake Magazine, Germ, Farther Stars Than These, Toasted Cheese* and *Headstuff*. Her debut collection, *Remember Me To The Bees*, is out now. Judy has a curious fondness for pigeons she can't quite explain and runs arts and literary blog. ‹SkyLightRain.com›

Karen S. Córdova is a writer and business woman who lives in California, but has deep roots in Colorado and New Mexico. She participates in spoken word performances, was featured in the *2010 Festival de Flor y Canto* at USC, and curated her first show, *Ekphrasis: Sacred Stories of the Southwest,* in 2014. Her book, *Farolito,* (3: A Taos Press, 2015), is a true story which casts a Hispano light on the dark subject of elder abuse and neglect, but also illuminates a jagged path to unexpected healing. Her favorite birds are Hummingbirds and Roadrunners. ‹karencordova.blogspot.com›

Nine-time Pushcart-Prize nominee and National Park Artist-in-Residence **Karla Linn Merrifield** has ten books to her credit; the newest are *Lithic Scatter and Other Poems* (Mercury Heartlink) and *Attaining Canopy: Amazon Poems* (FootHills Publishing). Forthcoming from FootHills is Bunchberries: More Poems of Canada, as sequel to her *Godwit: Poems of Canada* (FootHills), which received the Eiseman Award. She is assistant editor and poetry book reviewer for *The Centrifugal Eye*. Her favorite birds are the Harpy Eagle and Blue-Footed Boobies. ‹karlalinn.blogspot.com›

Kate Wells is an English teacher at a small charter high school in the foothills of the Sierra Nevada. She has been published in *Albatross, Rattlesnake Review* and *Ash Canyon Review*. She lives with her husband and their two remarkably tall children in a cabin by the river and still waffles on the Oxford Comma.

Katy Brown is a poet and photographer whose work appears online in *Medusa's Kitchen Blogspot* and *Convergence*. She has won awards in The Ina Coolbrith Circle, Berkeley Poets' Dinner, California Federation of Chaparral Poets, and The International Dance Poetry competitions. She was nominated for the Pushcart Prize. Her poetry has appeared in numerous journals and anthologies. Her secret power is that she can catch a lizard with a blade of grass. Her favorite bird is the Raven. <kbrown4081@aol.com>

Kimberly White's poetry has appeared in numerous journals and anthologies. She is the author of four chapbooks, *Penelope, A Reachable Tibet, The Daily Diaries of Death,* and *Letters To A Dead Man*; two novels: *Bandy's Restola,* and *Hotel Tarantula*. Find poetry and collage art on her website, as well as on Facebook and her boyfriend's refrigerator. <purplecouchworks.com>

Larry Schug lives with his wife, dog and three cats (who are tied up when outside, so they can't kill birds) near a large tamarack bog in St. Wendel Twp. Minnesota. His seventh book of poems, *At Gloaming,* from North Star Press was released in March 2014. He is retired from a life of various kinds of physical labor and volunteers as a writing tutor and naturalist.

Laurie Kolp lives in Southeast Texas and serves as president of Texas Gulf Coast Writers. She has been known to drop everything and bird-watch. In fact, Laurie once got lost from her group at the zoo while chasing cardinals, camera in hand. Her most recent publications include the *Concho River Review, 2015 Poet's Market, Blue Fifth Review, Pirene's Fountain*. Laurie's first full-length poetry collection is *Upon the Blue Couch* (Winter Goose Publishing, 2014). Her favorite bird is the Cardinal. <lauriekolp.com>

Lillo Way's poems have appeared (or are forthcoming) in *Poet Lore, The Madison Review, The Sow's Ear Poetry Review, Poetry East, Common Ground Review, Permafrost, Cordite Review* (Australia), *The Bear Deluxe* and others. She has received grants from the NEA, NY State Council on the Arts and the Geraldine R. Dodge Foundation for her choreographic work involving poetry. She has been a frequent reader on NPR's *Selected Shorts*. Lillo's favorite bird is the Hoopoe.

Linda M. Crate is a Pennsylvanian native born in Pittsburgh yet raised in the rural town of Conneautville. She currently resides in Meadville. Her poetry, short stories, articles, and reviews have been published in a myriad of magazines both online and in print. Recently her two chapbooks *A Mermaid Crashing Into Dawn* (Fowlpox Press, 2013) and *Less Than A Man* (The Camel Saloon, 2014) were published. Her fantasy novel *Blood & Magic* is forthcoming from Ravenswood Publishing. Her favorite bird is the Raven.

Linda Strever's poetry collection, *Against My Dreams,* was released in fall 2013. Her poetry credits include *Beloit Poetry Journal, CALYX Journal, Crab Creek Review, Floating Bridge Review, Nimrod, Spoon River Poetry Review, VoiceCatcher Journal* and others. Winner of the Lois Cranston Memorial Poetry Prize and a Pushcart Prize nominee, she has an MFA from Brooklyn College. When not writing, she sews art quilts and sings sea shanties. <LindaStrever.com>

Lois P. Jones is a host of L.A. radio's *Poet's Café*. Some publications include *Tupelo Quarterly, Narrative Magazine, The Warwick Review* and *American Poetry Journal* with upcoming work in *Eyewear* and *Texas University Press*. New Yorker staff writer Dana Goodyear selected "Ouija" as Poem of the Year (2010). Lois won the 2012 *Tiferet* Prize and the 2012 *Liakoura Prize* and is featured in *The Tiferet Talk Interviews* with Robert Pinsky. She is Poetry Editor of *Kyoto Journal*.

Lori Loranger practices mediation, tai chi, permaculture and civil disobedience on the Washington side of the Columbia River Gorge, where she's lived for over 30 years, along with a wide variety of local birds. Her poetry appears in *Ghost Town Poetry* anthologies volume 1 and 2 and *Visions of Light*. <lori@novah.org>

Lucy, made in Hong Kong, exported to the UK as a transracial adoptee. Lucy is a dyslexic British East Asian actor, filmmaker, author, nom de plume **Lucy Chau Lai-Tuen** and playwright. She loves dim sum, Yorkshire pudding and green tea. Her published works include: *Dance is New, Perpetual Child, Adoptionland, Adoption Therapy* and *Dear Wonderful You*. <LucySheen.com>

Lylanne Musselman is an award winning poet, playwright, and artist. Her work has appeared in *Pank, Flying Island, Literary Brushstrokes,* and *The Rusty Nail*, among others, and many anthologies. She is the author of three chapbooks and she co-authored *Company of Women: New and Selected Poems* (Chatter House Press, 2013). Presently, she teaches writing at Washtenaw Community College and Eastern Michigan University. Musselman lives in Toledo, Ohio, with her three cats, Graham, Tink, and Fiyero. Her favorite bird is the Northern Cardinal. <lylannemusselman.wordpress.com>

Lynn Knapp is a poet, memoirist, and teacher. She loves languages, second-language students, music, and of course, birds. Her poetry has most recently been published in *The Burden of Light*, an anthology edited by Tanya Chernov to benefit the National Colorectal Cancer Research Alliance. <lknapp094@gmail.com>

Lytton Bell has published five books: *A Path before Winter* (1998), *The Book of Chaps* (2002), *Nectar* (2011), *Poetica Erotica, Volume One* (2012), and *Body Image* (2013) and won seven poetry contests Her work has appeared in over six dozen publications. Lytton graduated magna cum laude from Bryn Mawr College. <lytton_bell@hotmail.com>

M is a Person. Poet. Performer. Sometimes even in that order. Her favorite bird is the Condor.

Co-author of the poetry collection *Fighting Monsters* (Melbourne, 1998) and the limited-edition artist's book *Golems Waiting Redux* (Portland, 2011), **M. F. McAuliffe** has contributed to *The Clarion Awards, Overland, Australian Short Stories, The Adelaide Review, Poezija* (Zagreb), and *Prairie Schooner*. In 2002 she co-founded Portland-based, multi-lingual *Gobshite Quarterly* with R.V. Branham; in 2008 they co-founded GobQ Books. She continues at both imprints as commissioning / contributing editor.

M.J.Iuppa lives on a small farm near the shores of Lake Ontario. *Between Worlds* is her most recent chapbook (Foothills Publishing, 2013). Recent poems, flash fictions, and essays appear in *When Women Waken, Poppy Road Review, Wild: A Quarterly, Eunoia Review, Andrea Reads America, Canto, Grey Sparrow Journal, The Poetry Storehouse, Avocet, Right Hand Pointing, Tiny-lights, The Lake (U.K.), The Kentucky Review*, and more. She is the Writer-in-Residence and Director of the Visual and Performing Arts Minor Program at St. John Fisher College. <mjiuppa.blogspot.com>

Madeline Levy is a Jersey bred, New Orleans transplant. She's been featured on afterhourspoetry.com, has well received blogs under varying pseudonyms, and has read her poems to half empty coffee shops across the east coast. She hates piña coladas, and getting caught in the rain. She's totally into yoga. Her favorite bird is Big Bird. <madelinecooperlevy@gmail.com>

Marcas mac an Tuairneir is a Gaelic writer of poetry, prose, drama and journalism, hailing from York. His début collection, *Deò* was published in 2013 by Grace Note Publications. A second, *Lus na Tùise,* is expected from the same in 2015. In 2014, he was awarded the Highland Literary Salon prize for poetry. Marcas lives in Inverness where he is a member of the local, award-winning Gaelic Choir and the Gaelic male-vocal group Trosg. His favorite bird is the Peacock. <MarcasMac.co.uk>

Maria Elena B. Mahler's poetry has been published internationally in English and Spanish in numerous presses and anthologies. Her first bilingual collection, *Sweeping Fossils* (Glass Lyre Press), will be released in 2016. She co-authored the non-fiction book *The Heart of Health* (Truth Publishing 2011) and is the editor of the poetry anthology *Woman in Metaphor* (NHH Press 2013). She was raised in Chile and now resides in the Sonora Desert of southern California.

Mariano Zaro is the author of four poetry books: *Where From/Desde Donde, Poems* *of Erosion/Poemas de la erosión*, *The House of Mae Rim/La casa de Mae Rim* and *Tres letras/Three Letters*. Most recently, *Buda en llamas/Buddha in Flames*, his Spanish translation of Tony Barnstone's poetry, was published in Mexico by El Tucán de Virginia. He earned a Ph.D. in Linguistics from the University of Granada (Spain). He teaches Spanish at Rio Hondo College (Whittier, California). His favorite bird is the Sparrow. <marianozaro.com>

Marie Lecrivain is the editor of *poeticdiversity: the litzine of Los Angeles*, a photographer, and a writer-in-residence at her apartment. She's been published in various journals, is the author of the alchemical chapbook *The Virtual Tablet of Irma Tre* (Edgar & Lenore's Publishing House, 2014), and her avocations include alchemy, fibre art, collecting various versions of Bronte novels, and long walks through the streets of Los Angeles.

Martie Odell-Ingebretsen was born in Pasadena, California. She received her AA degree at Pasadena City College and attended UC Berkeley and several California State College campuses where she majored in English Literature and Creative Writing. She is a child-development specialist and taught young children for over thirty years. Her Novella, *Sweet William* was published in 2013. She has written over two thousand poems, one of which was nominated for the Pushcart Prize. Martie lives in Sacramento. Her favorite birds are Peacocks and Peahens.

Mary Jo Balistreri has two full books of poetry, *Joy in the Morning* and *Gathering the Harvest* (Bellowing Ark Press) and a chapbook, *Best Brothers*, (Tiger's Eye Press). She has recent work in *Parabola, Grist, Plainsongs, Avocet, Crab Creek Review, Quill and Parchment* and others. *Poetrystorehouse* has offered videos of two of her poems. She has six Pushcart and two Best of the Net nominations. Mary Jo is one of the founders of Grace River Poets, an outreach for women's shelters, churches, and schools. Her favorite bird is the Hummingbird. <maryjobalistreripoet.com>

Mary Kay Rummel's seventh book of poetry, *The Lifeline Trembles*, has been published by Blue Light Press of San Francisco as a winner of the 2014 Blue Light Poetry Prize. Recent publications include poems in *Nimrod, Pirene's Fountain, St. Paul Almanac* and in the art book, *Woman in Metaphor* by Stephen Linsteadt. She teaches part time at California State University, Channel Islands and divides her time between Minnesota and California where she is the first Poet Laureate of Ventura County. Her favorite birds are the Cardinal and Great Blue Heron. <marykayrummel.com>

Mary Slocum, a shipyard electrician for 17 years with MSW (now retired), was the last winner of the Portland Artquake competition and a winner of a Washington State Poetry Assn. humorous poetry competition in the 90's. She has been published in *Stanza, NW Literary Review, Upper Left Edge, Black Cat*, and others. She enjoys reading publically more than publishing and has also appeared with a comedy collective. Her collection, *Greatest Hits: 60 Years of Lookin'* (Dancing Moon Press) is available in e-book form. Her favorite bird is the Raven. <maryslocum.com>

Marybeth Rua-Larsen spent several years volunteering at a Wildlife Rehabilitation Center patching up birds of prey, pigeons, crows, and other winged creatures in hopes of returning them to the wild. Her poems have appeared in *The Raintown Review, Cleaver, Measure* and *Unsplendid*. She won the 2011 Over the Edge New Writer of the Year Competition in Poetry in Galway, Ireland, and her chapbook *Nothing In-Between* was recently published by Barefoot Muse Press. Her favorite bird is the Black-Crowned Night Heron. <mrualarsen@comcast.net>

Matt Amott is a poet, photographer, a wanderer and charter member of the Pacific Vagabonds. As a co-founder of Six ft. Swells Poetry Press, most of his research and work for the press is done "in the field." His ramblings tend to favor the short poem due to the lack of space on the cocktail napkin. He has been published in numerous journals and reviews and his poems have been selected for the *Poems-For-All* Series in Sacramento and San Diego. Matt's favorite bird is the Owl. <afterhourspoetry.com>

Maureen O'Brien is the author of the novel *b-mother* (Houghton Mifflin Harcourt) and the chapbook *The Other Cradling* (Finishing Line Press). Her work has appeared in the *Redrock Review, The Louisville Review, Southern Women's Writer's Review, Referential Magazine* and is forthcoming in *Rhino*. Her poems have won first place in both the New Millennium Writing Awards and the Patricia Dobler Poetry Prize. She is getting closer to understanding what the birds are trying to tell her.

Melinda Palacio lives in Santa Barbara and New Orleans. Her house near Audubon Park in New Orleans is named *The Bird House* because of its location and the poet's love for birds. Her chapbook, *Folsom Lockdown*, won Kulupi Press' Sense of Place 2009 award. Her collection, *How Fire Is a Story, Waiting*, was a finalist for the 2013 Milt Kessler Award and the Paterson Prize. Recently, she was named a 2014 finalist for the Rita Dove Poetry Award and the 2014 Faulkner Wisdom Competition. Melinda's favorite bird is the Western Scrub Jay. <melindapalacio.com>

Mercedes Webb-Pullman: IIML Victoria University Wellington MA in Creative Writing 2011. Work online, in print (*Turbine, 4th Floor, Swamp, Reconfigurations, The Electronic Bridge, Otoliths, poetryrepairs, Connotations Press, The Red Room*, anthologies, her books (*Ono, Looking for Kerouac, After the Danse, Numeralla Dreaming, Food 4 Thought, Tasseography, Bravo Charlie Foxtrot* and *Collected poems 2008 - 2014*). Her favorite bird is the Cockatoo. <benchpress.co.nz>

Michael Shay was born in Germany, grew up in Chicago and studied at both the Undergraduate and Graduate Iowa Writers' Workshop in poetry. He received a Master of Creative Arts In Interdisciplinary and Experimental Art from San Francisco State (CEIA), and makes his living as a commercial photographer in Portland, OR. He has been a contributing editor to *The Alberta St. Anthology, Volume I and II* and has had work appear in *The Cape Rock, Nimrod International Journal of the Arts, Lullwater Review, The South Carolina Review* and *Rhino* among others.

Moya Roddy has published a novel, a collection of short stories, and her work has been produced on TV, radio and stage. Her collection *Other People* was long-listed for the prestigious Frank O'Connor Award and *Dance Ballerina Dance*, a radio play, was shortlisted for the PJ O'Connor Award. The Irish Times described her novel *The Long Way Home* as "simply brilliant." She maintains she used to be funny, out-going and talkative, but then she took up writing. One of her favorite birds is the Robin.

Parker Bauman is a Human Rights attorney, who pens poetry to keep her sanity. She has been published in *Connecticut River Review, Big Muddy* and *Earthen Lamp Journal*. She has a weird thing for crows and other feathered critters and finds a way to incorporate them into her poems. She lives in Connecticut but hopes to someday return to her first love, New Orleans, where she will live a long life of wordsmithery. Her favorite birds are Great Blue Herons and Cormorants.

Over the years of exhibiting her work, a combination of her poetry in calligraphic form and collages of paste paper, **Pattie Palmer-Baker** discovered (to her delight and surprise!) that most people, despite what they may believe, do like poetry, and in fact many like the poetry better than the visual art. She now concentrates on poetry. She still creates artwork but not as often. She finds poetry is more engaging. She loves words and her favorite bird is the Crow.

Pete Mullineaux lives in Galway, Ireland. He is widely published, including *Poetry Ireland Review 100* (Ed. Paul Muldoon) *The Stinging Fly, Van Gogh's Ear* (Paris) *Poetry Daily* & about.com/poetry (USA). Pete's work was featured recently on Irish national radio (ARENA – RTE Radio 1) and in *FUSION magazine,* Berklee College of Music, Boston. Three collections: *Zen Traffic Lights,* (Lapwing 2005) *A Father's Day* (Salmon Poetry 2008) and *Session* (Salmon Poetry 2011.) His favorite bird is the Long-Eared Owl.

Prize winning poet/artist, **Rachael Ikins** first published at age 14. Her 5th chapbook, *Historias* (Finishing Line Press) will soon join her others with her YA novel *The Complete Tales from the Edge of the Woods,* nominated for a 2013 CNY Book Award, on Amazon. Hummingbirds visit her balcony often with tree toads, and a sparrow she named 'Braveheart'. Her dogs and cat are her boon companions on moonlit adventures and made cameo appearances in *The Tales.* Her favorite bird is the Screech Owl. <rachaelikins.com>

Ram Krishna Singh, born, brought up and educated in Varanasi, is a university professor. He has authored over 160 academic articles, 170 book reviews, and 39 books, including *The River Returns* (2006), *Sexless Solitude and Other Poems* (2009), *Sense and Silence: Collected Poems* (2010), *New and Selected Poems Tanka and Haiku* (2012), and *I Am No Jesus and Other Selected Poems, Tanka and Haiku* (2014). <pennyspoetry.wikia.com/wiki/R.K._Singh>

Richard King Perkins II is a state-sponsored advocate for residents in long-term care facilities. He has a wife, Vickie and a daughter, Sage. He is a three-time Pushcart nominee and a Best of the Net nominee whose work has appeared in hundreds of publications including *The Louisiana Review, Bluestem, Emrys Journal, The Red Cedar Review* and more. He has poems forthcoming in *The Roanoke Review, The Alembic* and *Milkfist.*

Robert R. Sanders has won over three dozen international awards in creative design, animation, and photography. He was nominated for an Emmy for *Fire Mountain*, a news documentary detailing the eruption of Mount. St. Helens. Robert's work spans half a century of creative development through an analog and digital journey. He's a teacher to thousands of aspiring artists, while always remaining a student of the light. His favorite bird is the Owl. <RobertSandersPhoto.com>

A socialist Laz poet-author from Turkey, **Serkan Engin** was born in 1975 in Izmit, Turkey. He published a poem manifesto, entitled *Imagist Socialist Poetry* (2004). He has been trying to launch a new movement in Turkish poetry and to this end has published numerous articles about literary theory. His poems and essays have been published in English in many international literary journals and also some of his poems appeared in Japanese in the leading Japanese philosophy and poetry journal *Shi to Shisou*.

Born and raised in New York, **Sharon Alexander** now lives in Southern California dividing her time between the mountains in Idyllwild and in the desert at the foot of the beautiful Santa Rosa Mountains. Sharon's first collection of poetry is *Voodoo Trombone* (Finishing Line Press, 2014). Her work has appeared in various journals including *Pearl, Slipstream, Crate, Tiger's Eye* and *Pinyon*. In addition, her poetry in included in the David St. John Anthology *Beyond the Lyric Moment* and in the art and poetry anthology *Woman in Metaphor*. <sharonalexanderpoetry.com>

In March, 2015 **Sharon Chmielarz**'s ninth book of poetry will be published, *Visibility: Ten Miles, a Prairie Memoir in Photography and Poetry*. Both the photographer and poet present inside views on the prairie, Ken Smith lives in North Dakota and Sharon grew up in South Dakota. She has new poems forthcoming or currently in *Ascent, Epoch, Louisiana Literature, Whistling Shade, Commonweal, Poetry East, Midwest Review* and Nodin Press's 2015 anthology of Minnesota poets. Her favorite bird is the Robin. <sharonchmielarz.com>

Sharon Lask Munson grew up in Detroit, Michigan. After college she taught school in England, Germany, Okinawa, and Puerto Rico before driving to Anchorage, Alaska where she put down roots and taught for the next twenty years. She is the author of the chapbook, *Stillness Settles Down the Lane* (Uttered Chaos Press, 2010), a full-length book of poems, *That Certain Blue* (Blue Light Press, 2011), and *Braiding Lives*, (Poetica Publishing Company, 2014). She lives and writes in Eugene, Oregon, and her favorite bird is the Ptarmigan. <sharonlaskmunson.com>

Shawn Aveningo is a globally published poet whose work has appeared in over 80 literary journals & anthologies, including *poeticdiversity: the litzine of Los Angeles*, who recently nominated her work for a Pushcart. She is the cofounder of The Poetry Box® and web-designer for *VoiceCatcher: a journal of women's voices & visions*. Shawn, a proud mother of three, has overcome her lifetime fear of birds and become quite fond of the black-eyed juncos that visit her backyard in Beaverton, Oregon. <redshoepoet.com>

Stephen Linsteadt is a painter, poet, and writer. His poetry is published in *Moments of the Soul* (Spirit First), *Cradle Songs* (Quill and Parchment Press), *Saint Julian Press, Pirene's Fountain, Synesthesia Literary Journal*, the *San Diego Poetry Annual*, and others. Stephen is the founder of Scalar Heart Connection and author of the book with the same title, which is concerned with humanity's connection, or lack thereof, with Nature, the Earth, and the global community. His favorite bird is the White Crane. <StephenLinsteadt.com>

Steve Williams lives and works in Portland with a lovely woman who writes and edits much better than he but refuses to admit it. Together, they host the Figures of Speech reading series at In Other Words feminist community center, are co-chairs of the Portland Unit of the Oregon Poetry Association, and attend as many poetry events as they can get to. Steve likes to support online journals and thus has most of his work in places like *Stirring, The Rose and Thorn, Word Riot* and other on-line journals.

Stuart A. Paterson, born 1966, lives by the sea in SW Scotland and writes poetry in English & Scots. His work has been widely published in anthologies, reviews & newspapers worldwide. *Saving Graces*, a collection from Poetry Scotland, was released in 1997. He received a Robert Louis Stevenson Fellowship from the Scottish Book Trust in 2014, and is fascinated by owls, the ivory billed woodpecker & the play of light through ambered glass. His favorite bird is the Laughing Owl (now extinct).

Susan G. Duncan is presently a consultant with a performing and visual arts clientele, capping a long career in arts administration. She served as executive director for San Francisco's musical comedy phenomenon *Beach Blanket Babylon*, the al fresco California Shakespeare Theater, and the Grammy-winning, all-male vocal ensemble Chanticleer. Her work has appeared in *Atlanta Review, Blast Furnace, Compass Rose, the G.W. Review, The MacGuffin, OmniArts, Poem, River Oak Review,* and *Thema,* among others. Her favorite bird is the American Dipper.

Sylvia Ashby's background is in theatre, acting and writing; she's published 15 plays for family audiences — with thousands of productions. About a year ago, she began sending out poetry, now has a few dozen pieces out or coming out: *Abyss & Apex, Pantheon, Rhino, Constellations, Subterranean,* as well as *Hermes* (UK), *Frostwriting* (Sweden), *Earthen Lamp* (India). Her favorite birds are Robins. <sylviaashby.com>

Taylor Graham is a volunteer search-and-rescue dog handler in the California Sierra and helps her husband, Hatch (a retired wildlife biologist/forester) with his bird projects. She's included in the anthologies *Villanelles* (Everyman's Library) and *California Poetry: From the Gold Rush to the Present* (Santa Clara University). Her latest book is *What the Wind Says* (Lummox Press, 2013), poems about living and working with her canine search partners over the past 40 years.

Tim Kahl is the author of *Possessing Yourself* (CW Books, 2009) and *The Century* *of Travel* (CW Books, 2012). His work has been published in *Prairie Schooner, Indiana Review, Sein und Werden, Notre Dame Review, , Konundrum Engine Literary Magazine, Parthenon West Review* and many other journals. He appears as Victor Schnickelfritz at the poetry and poetics blog *The Great American Pinup* and the poetry video blog *Linebreak Studios*. He is also editor of Bald Trickster Press and Clade Song. He is the vice president and events coordinator of The Sacramento Poetry Center. <timkahl.com>

Todd Cirillo is co-founder and editor of Six Ft. Swells Press. He is one of the originators of the After-Hours Poetry movement. Todd's books include *Sucker's Paradise, Everybody Knows the Dice Are Loaded, Still a Party, This Troubled Heart, ROXY,* and *Tonight, You're Coming Home With Us* which he co-authored. Todd lives in New Orleans, Louisiana where he soaks his pirate heart in rum, second line parades, the Mississippi river, and twisted love under the neons. His favorite bird is the Wild Turkey. <afterhourspoetry.com>

Tricia Knoll is a Portland, Oregon poet who feeds birds daily. One stellar jay has her at its beck and call. Her chapbook *Urban Wild* came out in 2014 from Finishing Line Press, focusing on interactions between wild creatures and humans in urban habitat. Her work has appeared in dozens of journals including *CALYX Journal*, the literary blog of *Columbia Journal*, and *Windfall – A Journal of Place*. Tricia's favorite bird is the Cardinal. <triciaknoll.com>

Vivien Jone's first poetry collection, *About Time, Too*, was published by Indigo Dreams Publishing (2010). In that year she also won the Poetry London Prize. She completed a second short fiction collection, *White Poppies* (2012), with the aid of a Creative Scotland Writer's Bursary and has adapted two of the stories for theatre performance in 2013. Her first eBook, *Malta Child*, is a memoir of four childhood years in Malta in the late 1950s. Her second poetry collection is *Short of Breath* (Cultured Llama Press, 2014). Her favorite bird is the Merlin. <vivienjones.info>

Birds of a Feather ...

Yes, we've all heard the expression, "Birds of a feather, flock together." And that's fine for geese or 80's rock bands named after seagulls, but what about those species of birds that don't necessarily *flock*? Through the years, man has managed to bestow some interesting, and sometimes downright silly, names to identify the social collectives of our fine, feathered friends. Some of these terms are commonly used in everyday language, while others are lesser known. A number of the collective nouns are quite complimentary, and some may seem a bit more derogatory. Regardless, they all give a nod to our human creativity, as well as deep-rooted affinity for relating to our natural world. So, for fun, take a gander and see how many of these collective terms you recognize:

Bitterns – a sedge or siege
Buzzards – a wake
Bobolinks – a chain
Chickens – a brood
Coots – a cover
Cormorants – a gulp
Crows – a murder or horde
Dotterel – a trip
Doves – a dule or pitying (specific to turtle doves)
Ducks – a brace, team, flock (in flight), raft (on water), paddling or badling
Eagles – a convocation
Finches – a charm
Flamingos – a stand
Geese – a flock, gaggle (on the ground) or skein (in flight)
Grouse – a pack (in late season)
Hawks – a cast, kettle (in flight) or boil (two or more spiraling in air)
Herons – a sedge or siege
Jays – a party or scold
Lapwings – a deceit
Larks – an exaltation
Mallards – a sord (in flight) or brace
Magpies – a tiding, gulp, murder or charm
Nightingales – a watch
Owls – a parliament
Parrots – a pandemonium or company

Partridge – a covey
Peacocks – an ostentation or muster
Penguins – a colony, muster, parcel or rookery
Pheasant – a nest, nide (a brood), nye or bouquet
Plovers – a congregation or wing (in flight)
Ptarmigans – a covey
Rooks – a building
Quail – a bevy or covey
Ravens – an unkindness or storytelling
Snipe – a walk or wisp
Sparrows – a host
Starlings – a murmuration
Storks – a mustering
Swans – a bevy, game or wedge (in flight)
Teal – a spring
Turkeys – a rafter or gang
Vultures – a colony
Woodcocks – a fall
Woodpeckers – a descent

Bird Index

The following birds appear by name in poem(s) which begin on the annotated page number(s):

Barn Owl: 69
Black-Necked Stilt: 16
Blackbird: 29, 71, 138
Blackbird (Red-Winged): 42, 47, 127
Booby: 68
Bulpul: 19
Cardinal: 42, 74, 82, 134
Caribbean Chuchubi: 93
Cassowary: 124
Chickadee: 42, 69, 109, 118
Chicken: 68, 85
Chough: 148
Cockatoo: 87, 126
Crane: 28, 29
Crow: 38, 54, 55, 56, 58, 61, 63, 64, 65, 80, 100, 147
Cuckoo: 126
Curlew: 33
Daw (Jackdaw): 64
Dodo: 68, 99
Dove: 64, 121
Dove (Mourning): 36, 80, 110, 142
Dove (Ring-Necked): 120,
Dove (Rock): 132
Duck (Brown): 135
Duck (Mallard): 127, 129
Eagle: 119, 145
Eagle (Golden): 123
Eagle (Harpy): 92
Egret: 29
Finch: 118, 138
Flamingo: 16
Fulmar: 148

Galah (Rose-Breasted Cockatoo): 138
Gannet: 148
Goldfinch: 41
Goose: 24, 71, 119
Goose (Canada): 26, 127
Goose (Pink-footed): 46
Grackle: 118
Grebe: 72
Gull: 42, 65, 80
Hawk: 42, 120, 121
Hawk (Red-Tailed): 147
Hen: 71
Heron: 33, 126, 147
Heron (Great Blue): 152
Hummingbird: 22, 75, 104, 105, 106, 107, 108
Hwamei: 126
Jay: 74, 110
Kenspeckle: 75
Kestrel: 148
Magpie: 64
Manx: 148
Merlin: 72
Mockingbird: 74
Mynah: 19
Northern Flicker: 142
Owl: 53, 54, 71
Owl (Great Horned): 16, 136
Oystercatcher: 33
Parrot: 19, 87, 113
Peacock: 68
Penguin: 68, 78
Peregrine Falcon: 95
Pheasant: 48, 118
Phoenix: 149
Pigeon: 19, 50, 71, 74, 83, 84, 89, 90, 95
Pigeon (Band-Tailed): 33
Pigeon (Homing): 44, 115, 116

Pigeon (Passenger): 98
Pigeon (Wood): 64
Raven: 34, 60, 64, 147
Robin: 42, 43, 74, 77, 110, 118, 131, 137
Rook: 64, 71
Seagull: 71, 145
Shag: 148
Shearwater: 148
Sparrow: 19, 21, 42, 52, 71, 74, 110, 114, 118, 131, 138, 147
Spoonbill: 16
Starling: 126
Stork: 16, 21, 148
Swallow: 67, 91
Swallow (African): 93
Swan: 31
Thrush (Violet): 126
Troupial: 93
Tui: 138
Vulture: 19, 100
Wheatear: 148
Woodpecker: 16, 45, 118, 146
Wren: 142

About The Poetry Box® / Flight Plans

The Poetry Box® was founded in 2011 by Shawn Aveningo & Robert R. Sanders, who whole-heartedly believe that every day spent with the people you love, doing what you love, is a moment in life worth celebrating.

It all started out as our way to help people memorialize the special milestones in their lives by melding custom poems with photographic artwork for anniversaries, birthdays, holidays and other special occasions. Robert and Shawn expanded on their shared passion for creating poetry and art with the introduction of The Poetry Box® Book Publishing.

Their fourth published book, *Poeming Pigeons – Poems about Birds*, has been a true labor of love, so much so that they decided to evolve it into *The Poeming Pigeon – A Literary Journal of Poetry*. They'll be publishing two themed journals a year, with Homer, *The Poeming Pigeon* mascot, taking flight to deliver poems to poetry lovers across the globe. Details and submission guidelines can be found at www.ThePoemingPigeon.com.

Robert and Shawn continue to celebrate the talents of their fellow artisans and writers. In addition to publishing two themed journals per year, The Poetry Box® now offers professional book design and publishing services to poets looking to publish their collections of poems and authors looking to publish novels, memoirs and creative non-fiction.

And as always, The Poetry Box® believes in giving back to the community. Each month a portion of all sales will benefit a different charity. For a complete list of the charities currently supported, please visit the Giving Back page on their website at www.ThePoetryBox.com.

Feel free to visit The Poetry Box® online bookstore, where you'll find more books including:

Keeping It Weird: Poems & Stories of Portland, Oregon

Verse on the Vine: A Celebration of Community, Poetry, Art & Wine

The Way a Woman Knows by Carolyn Martin

Order Form

Need more copies for friends and family? No problem. We've got you covered with two convenient ways to order:

1. Go to our website at www.thePoetryBox.com and click on Bookstore.

or

2. Fill out the order form. Email it to Shawn@thePoetryBox.com or mail it to: The Poetry Box, 2228 NW 159th Pl, Beaverton, OR 97006.

Name: _____

Shipping Address: _____

_____

Phone Number: (____) _____

Email Address: _____ @ _____

Payment Method: __Cash __Check __PayPal Invoice __Credit Card

Credit Card #: _____ CCV _____

Expiration Date: _____ Signature: _____

Poeming Pigeons – Poems about Birds - # of Copies: _____

x $15.00: _____

Plus Shipping & Handling: _____
($3 per book, or $7.95 for 3 or more books)

Order Total: _____

Thank You!

Made in the USA
San Bernardino, CA
19 April 2015